P54317

LAW AND SOCIETY

BLANDFORD
SOCIAL STUDIES SERIES

General Editor: Paul Mathias

*Formerly Advisory Teacher in the Social Sciences
to the Inner London Education Authority.
Deputy Headmaster, Upton House School,
Hackney, London.*

THE TEACHER'S HANDBOOK FOR
SOCIAL STUDIES
Paul Mathias

1
HEREDITY AND ENVIRONMENT
Joseph Dunthorn

2
FAMILY AND KINSHIP
Norah Cook

3
GROUPS AND COMMUNITIES
Paul Mathias

4
MASS MEDIA AND THEIR SOCIAL EFFECTS
Reginald Holme

5
LAW AND SOCIETY
Peter Bulwer

LAW
AND
SOCIETY

PETER BULWER

BLANDFORD PRESS
POOLE DORSET

EDITOR'S NOTE

This series of books caters particularly for pupils aged between 13 and
16, including those taking C.S.E. examinations, but they may also be
found useful for pupils in other age groups studying these topics,
either as part of Social Studies courses, as part of more general work in
the Humanities, or in integrated studies.

In this book Peter Bulwer, Head of Humanities at Forest School,
Horsham, Sussex, has provided a lot of information about many
aspects of law and procedure and their relationship to society which are
frequently studied and for which very little detailed material is
available at this level.

The sections on the work of solicitors, barristers and on the courts are
clearly written and should be found particularly valuable. Because of
the nature of many legal terms which must be used, a glossary has
been included in this book, although it is not the general policy for the
series.

We would like to acknowledge the generous help given by many people
in the preparation of this book: Peter North, Advisory Teacher in the
Social Sciences to the Inner London Education Authority, and Sean
Bourke, Lecturer in Sociology at Isleworth Polytechnic who read the
manuscript in its early stages and made valuable comments and
suggestions; Howard Dingwall, LLB, a recently called barrister of
Lincoln's Inn who contributed material on several aspects of law
procedure including the trial case on pages 39–40; The Scottish Law
Society and George Williamson, SSC (Solicitor to the Supreme Courts
in Scotland) who advised on the Scottish Legal System; and Richard
Murray, Barrister in Liverpool, who read the manuscript and made
helpful comments. We would also like to thank Miss Constance Smith,
former Headmistress of Penrhos College, Colwyn Bay, for the
Assignment on Socrates at the end of Section 1.

© Blandford Press Ltd, 1975
Link House, West Street, Poole, Dorset, BH15 1LL

ISBN 0 7137 3358 6

Printed in Great Britain by
Butler & Tanner Ltd,
Frome and London

CONTENTS

Editor's Note   *page* 4

1 Order in Society   7

2 Some Differing Legal Systems   14

3 The English Legal System   19

4 How Legal Systems in Britain Work   28

5 Law Enforcement   43

6 Sentences and Treatment of Offenders   50

7 The Law in Action   59

8 Law in a Changing Society   66

Glossary   69

General References   70

For Further Reading   70

Acknowledgements   71

Index   71

The Law Courts in the Strand, London

The Assembly held by the boys in *Lord of the Flies*. (Taken from the film)

1
ORDER IN SOCIETY

LAWS

In the book *Lord of the Flies* by William Golding, a group of boys are stranded on a desert island. One of them, Piggy, wants laws made by an assembly to control things. The others don't agree—at first. Why was it necessary for them—and why is it necessary for us—to have laws?

The word LAW comes from the same root as LAY—that is, those who first began to make law did so to lay the basis for living together happily and making a society. The dictionary defines LAW as 'a body of enacted or customary rules recognised as binding'. Law, to be binding or effective, must be recognised by the community as a whole and agreed to by them.

Some find rules irritating, especially when they can't see the reason for them. Yet rules and laws are needed in all societies. The important thing is to realise that the law is not something imposed from outside, but an agreed way of living together. You can't play football unless both sides are agreed on the 'rules of the game'. And a people or nation cannot live happily together as a community, unless the majority agree on the 'rules of their common life'.

Laws regulate the rights and duties that are important for the life of the whole group; that is, those which affect the COMMON GOOD. They also protect the rights and decide the duties of the individual; this

can be called the PRIVATE GOOD. Laws limit what an individual can do that might harm others, and they also set limits on what society can do that might harm individuals. So laws are ways of reducing the conflict that can exist between the many and various interests of people making up a group or society. This conflict is found in all societies and groups, and sometimes the balance moves like a see-saw. At times the weight is so firmly on the side of society that the interests of the individual or a minority group seem to be forgotten; at other times an individual or small group may have so much power that they control all the laws to their own benefit and ignore the interests of most people.

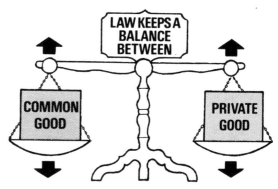

The laws of a country are often the result of customs or rules of conduct that have grown up over a long period of time. Some have their basis in moral and religious laws.

Moral laws

The keeping of moral laws is a matter of individual and group conscience. Each person must decide what action to take when each choice between right and wrong appears. As we have seen, social laws are agreed rules of behaviour set out for the good of the community and of the people in it. People can decide whether or not to obey any law of society that affects them, but society has the right and the power to demand obedience to its laws, and to enforce them by the threat of punishment as a penalty for disobedience.

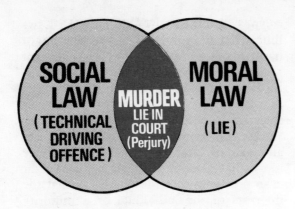

SOCIAL LAW (TECHNICAL DRIVING OFFENCE) — MURDER LIE IN COURT (Perjury) — MORAL LAW (LIE)

the earliest law codes known to man—that of Hammurabi of Babylonia some 4,000 years ago. Such early codes made no difference between the Law, moral law and laws of religion; for all were regarded as coming from the God to whom the community believed it owed its origin and continued existence.

Religious laws

This term covers both social laws and moral laws, and also a number of rituals belonging to different religions. So Jewish men and women keep their hats on and take their shoes off when they go into a holy place or attend a religious ceremony such as a funeral. Muslims also remove their shoes on entering a mosque (their holy place) and wash their hands, feet and faces before starting to pray. A Hindu can explain why a cow is sacred. A Jain brushes the ground before his feet as he walks and covers his mouth with a cloth, because he must not take life, even that of the smallest insect. There are hundreds more examples. They are the accepted rules of the religious community to which they apply, and usually very strictly kept.

Although laws vary considerably between different societies, there are three main areas in all societies in which human conduct has to be regulated:

Territory
Ownership
Personal relationships

Many moral laws become part of social law. For example, the moral laws 'Thou shalt not steal' and 'Thou shalt do no murder' are included in the Law of nearly every human society. Both appear in one of

Hammurabi gave decisions on disputes, based on those given by earlier kings in similar cases. These are called precedents. If no precedent existed, Hammurabi had to make decisions. All these decisions were recorded on clay tablets. This stone monument was set up and listed over 282 laws.

8

Territory

All societies find it necessary to have clearly defined rules concerning their rights for hunting, fishing, feeding herds and cultivating crops. This is necessary for survival. Territorial rules are strict in such societies as the Hopi Indians of Northern Arizona and the Mbuti Pygmies of Africa (see *Groups and Communities* by Paul Mathias in this series).

These rules differ according to the environment. In England the rights of those cultivating crops were protected from damage by animals by the law which made it the duty of those owning animals to fence them in. If not they would have to pay compensation for any damage caused. But in the USA, with its wide prairie regions, this would not be practical. There the grower of the crops must fence his land to prevent animals from eating or damaging them. This reflects the size of the ranches.

Territorial rights can also mean survival of another kind: the need to defend the boundaries against an outside aggressor. Many wars have been fought over land ownership. A war can result in the re-drawing of boundaries and whole groups of people may find themselves governed by the laws of another country. This happened in the First and Second World Wars.

Countries define their boundaries very clearly. Points of exits and entrance are marked and controlled. Movement of people and goods is carefully checked. Only certain types of money and goods may be taken from one country to another. Customs posts are familiar to anyone travelling abroad today, and so are passports, or visas. It is also as well to learn something of the laws of the country to which you are going. In some they are much more severe than others, and what may seem a small offence may involve several years imprisonment according to the laws of the country you are visiting.

Ownership
Some societies lay stress on individual ownership and inheritance. Laws about ownership are very complicated. Laws on inheritance, whether it is of property or wealth, vary a great deal.

Other societies, such as socialist countries like the USSR, have common (or state) ownership. In the USSR laws about theft (taking something that does not belong to you) are very severe.

Examples of borders being changed after the Balkan War

Marriage

'Marriage' as an institution is found in most societies. The laws which govern it vary considerably from country to country and from century to century.

Laws concerning the age at which two people are allowed to marry differ widely. Sometimes the consent of the parents is a deciding factor.

Some societies allow only a monogamous marriage, that is one man to one woman. Some societies allow polygamous marriages—for example, Muslim societies allow a man up to four wives and some tribes in the Himalayas allow a woman several husbands. In most cases the reasons for this are economic. For example, in some rural communities it is an asset to have more than one partner and many children (see *Family and Kinship* by Norah Cook in this series).

Laws concerning divorce also vary from country to country, as do those concerning the custody of the children in these circumstances.

Underlying these variations are a whole series of religious, moral, social and economic factors which are closely linked with the idea of safeguarding the family and society. Questions such as ownership of property and money are involved. Proceedings have to be according to the law of the land.

There can be complications when families from one society move into a country where there are different laws on marriage and divorce. For example, a Muslim who has already one, two or three wives before entering Britain is legally married to them all. But if he has married once and wants to marry again while in England, this is illegal according to English laws, though it would be legal according to his Muslim law. Muslim laws are both religious laws and also the official state laws of the countries where the Muslim religion is the state religion.

The Rule of Law

The idea of the Rule of Law probably began in Greek and Roman times, in the belief that human happiness needed an ordered society and that this was only possible under the Rule of Law.

In England the idea that the Law was above all came to the front in the thirteenth century when it was said 'The King himself ought not to be subject to any man, but he should be subject to God and the Law, for the Law makes him King.'

This idea gradually developed into the modern version of the Rule of Law. In the nineteenth century a great English legal writer called Albert Dicey said that the Rule of Law meant three things:

1. The regular law of the land is more powerful than any government and all governments must obey it.
2. All people of any rank or class are subject to the law and are equal in the eyes of the law and before its courts.
3. The law of the constitution itself is based upon the rights of individuals as declared by the courts.

Point 1 acts as protection against the government using power harmfully, since a government's acts must be within the Law.

Point 2 guarantees equality to everyone, rich and poor, young and old, man and woman, weak and strong.

Point 3 guarantees personal freedom. In England, for example, people may only be arrested according to the law. If arrested, they may not be kept in custody unless they are charged. Even then, they must be released unless sufficient evidence is brought to prove their guilt. (In legal terms, this is through a writ of *Habeas Corpus*.) In an emergency this can be altered.

The idea of the Rule of Law, although it has changed slightly from the original ideas of Dicey, is still the basis of the legal system in England and many countries.

The International Court at The Hague

INTERNATIONAL LAW

Sometimes known as the Law of Nations, International Law developed and became more important in the eighteenth and nineteenth centuries because of changes in world society. The lessening of the Pope's authority together with the emergence and growth of strong governments and the new dimension of world affairs brought about by the spread of colonies, all increased the need for international regulation.

The increase of international trade has led to active co-operation between states. An example of this is the international conferences which take place about shipping and the carriage of goods.

International Law may be divided into two parts:
1 Private International Law concerning the disputes between individuals of different nations. In this case the dispute is usually settled in one of the courts of one of the nations involved.
2 Public International Law concerning the disputes between nations. It also includes laws relating to nationality, extradition, patents and trade marks. Although there is no over-riding authority, cases under International Law have been heard by the International Court at The Hague in the Netherlands. This is the Court of the

Judges of the International Court at work

United Nations and countries which have signed its Charter are parties to it and should accept its authority.

The basic principles of International Law are:

1 Recognition of each other's existence and integrity as states.
2 Recognition of each other's independence.
3 Recognition of the equality of all independent states.

Most nations accept these principles, but there are some cases where they have not been kept.

The International Court of Justice at The Hague

This was set up shortly after the Second World War to bring about a system of settling disputes between sovereign states. It is the permanent and main judicial body of the United Nations and made up of fifteen judges who are elected for nine years by the General Assembly and the Security Council of the United Nations. There are provisions to prevent the elections from being involved with political questions. The electors must keep in mind the importance of the judges being representative of the different legal systems and societies in the world.

At least nine judges must be sitting to hear a case presented to the Court. The Court reads pleadings (written or printed statements) presented by the parties concerned and hears the arguments of their lawyers. Judgements are given in both English and French, which are the official languages of the Court. The decision of the Court carries great weight and is usually accepted.

One case submitted to the International Court in 1974 by the United Kingdom concerned a claim by Iceland that they were entitled to extend their zone of exclusive fisheries jurisdiction to 50 nautical miles. Iceland, which depends largely on fishing for its trade, felt very keenly about this issue. There were many items in the newspapers and other mass media about Icelandic patrol boats seeking to exclude UK and German fishing vessels.

Iceland did not consider this a case for the International Court and did not take part when it came up. Despite this, the case was heard and the Court made an interim judgement that the government of Iceland was not entitled to exclude UK fishing vessels from the disputed areas.

Some of the Secretariat of the International Court

FOR INVESTIGATION AND DISCUSSION

1 Which is better, to have rules and agree or to hurt and kill. Piggy in *Lord of the Flies* wants rules. Do you? Discuss.

2 Try to imagine life in a community without laws or rules and with complete freedom for each person. What problems would this create?

3 Show how difficulties may arise when people from a different society go to live in another society with different customs and laws.

4 Find out what you can about early law codes such as those of the Hammurabi. How have some of these survived until today? How were they decided upon and what was their origin?

5 If you disobey a moral law, against which there is no legal penalty, can you expect to get away with it scotfree or does it have consequences? If so, what sort of consequences?

6 Discuss stealing from the angle of 'right and wrong'. Is society justified in making laws to punish theft?

7 Discuss dishonesty from the same angles. What kinds of conduct do you think are dishonest? How many of these come under the Law as far as you know, and are punishable if committed? How far can society enforce honesty and prevent dishonesty?

8 When Socrates, a Greek thinker, was condemned to death on charges of leading young people astray and not believing in the gods, his friends urged him to escape. He felt that if one believed in the idea of Law, and the Law gives the death penalty, it would not be keeping the Law to evade its sentence by escaping.

He said to his friends:

'Suppose that while we were preparing to run away from here, the Laws and Constitution were to come and confront us with the question: 'Can you deny that by this act you intend, so far as you have the power to destroy us, the Laws and the whole State as well? Do you imagine a City can continue to exist and not be turned upside down if the legal judgements which are pronounced in it have no force but are nullified and destroyed by private persons?'... Should we reply, 'Yes, I do intend to destroy the laws because the State wronged me by passing a faulty judgement at my trial?'

From this, discuss the following points:

(a) Does the disobedience to the laws destroy a state?
(b) Why should the laws of a country be obeyed?
(c) Should all laws be treated with equal respect?
(d) Is it ever desirable to break the laws of a country? If so, in what circumstances?
(e) Would Socrates have been right to escape if in so doing he went against his principles in upholding the Law?

9 In what ways has International Law been broken recently?

2
SOME DIFFERING LEGAL SYSTEMS

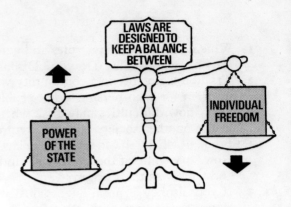

Basic Freedoms
Most people would stress the importance of everyone having:

1. freedom to vote and elect representatives of different parties
2. freedom from arrest without charge or trial
3. freedom of speech
4. freedom of the press
5. freedom of assembly, meeting and holding processions.

This basic list can be kept in mind as we look at different systems of law operating in several countries.

Democratic systems of government
As we have seen, there can be a clash between the freedom of the individual and the interests of the community. In democratic countries, the law and constitution guarantee personal freedom. It is possible to criticise the system of democracy, or even democracy itself, but at least in democratic countries people elect their own representatives to Parliament. So they should accept the Rule of Law and work for bad or out-of-date laws to be changed or removed.

A legal maxim (saying) is that 'justice should not only be done, it should be seen to be done'. This can be said to apply in democratic countries. Individuals and groups can usually make sure that they are treated with justice. Although individuals may sometimes have cause to complain, the law works well on the whole.

Even in a democracy, however, people and their elected representatives must always be on the alert to see that the laws are just and being carried out, and that the freedom of people is not whittled away by government regulations.

In the Western world there are countless systems of law, but they spring from two main roots: English Common Law or Roman Law. These roots are also the basis of law in some non-Western countries.

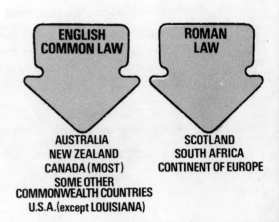

Different countries not only have different systems of law and organisation of the courts, but there is also a great variation in the importance given to the freedom of the individual and the idea of justice. This contrast is seen in its most extreme form in the difference between democratic and totalitarian systems of government.

Totalitarian systems of government

If a nation has a dictatorship or any form or totalitarian government, it is unlikely that the individual will enjoy real freedom or have much influence in government. There may not be free elections for all people and there may be imprisonment without charge or trial.

In this type of system the law is often used as a political weapon to support the government in power and to crush the opponents rather than as something to ensure the rights of all citizens. Extreme Right-Wing or Left-Wing governments may use the law to remove their political opponents. Freedom of the individual is not regarded as of any great importance. The welfare of the State overrules all other considerations.

We will take a look at examples of legal systems in a democratic government and a totalitarian government.

United States of America (USA)

The USA is a federation of fifty states. There are two systems of laws and courts—one State and one Federal. These systems are based on English law, with one exception: the state of Louisana was settled originally by the French and its State law is based on Roman law.

State laws may vary from state to state. A crime in one state may not be considered a crime in another. Even for a motoring offence a man may not be liable to a charge after crossing the border to another state. Arrest for more serious offences may be avoided by crossing the state line in some cases.

Federal law deals with:

cases between citizens of different federal states
cases involving the Constitution
admiralty cases
cases in which the USA is a party.

Since the American system has grown up from the English system of law, it is understandable that the *Habeas Corpus* writ has been adopted to protect citizens from arbitrary arrest and imprisonment. It is written into the Constitution and observed by both Federal and State Law. The other basic freedoms are also written into the Constitution, but with this division between Federal and State Law there can be varieties of interpretation.

The USA is a democratic country and, as with all democracies, her laws can be changed. Bills affecting these changes have to be passed through Congress.

Her legal system is divided as follows:

Federal judiciary
This consists of three sets of Federal Courts.

A court scene in the USA taken from the film *Anatomy of a Murder*
What difference do you note between this and British courts?

15

The Supreme Court, which is at Washington D.C., has a Chief Justice and eight Associate Justices. It is largely a court of appeal from lower Federal Courts and from the Supreme Courts of the States.

The United States Courts of Appeal which deal with appeals from the Federal District Courts.

Ninety-three District Courts which are served by 340 District Court Judges and deal with cases involving Federal Law.

State judiciaries

These vary slightly from state to state but are generally of three types.

The State Supreme Courts, called Courts of Appeal in some states, which hear appeals from lower State Courts.

The State Superior Courts, known as District Courts or Circuit Courts in some states, which are concerned with all the more serious and important cases under State Law.

Justices of the Peace Courts, which are lower courts dealing with the less serious and less important cases.

There are sometimes cases where there is a dispute in law between one state and another, or between a state and the Federal Government. In these cases the Federal Supreme Court has the final say.

The Union of Soviet Socialist Republics (USSR)

Like the USA, the USSR is a federation and has both Federal and State Courts. The Supreme Court of the USSR is the final authority. Special Courts of the USSR deal with more serious cases. There are State Courts for the various republics and regions, and People's Courts which are local courts where the less serious cases are tried.

Each People's Court has a full-time judge who sits with two locally elected assessors, not legally trained, a little similar to Justices of the Peace. These courts are supposed to educate the people and so the cases are usu-

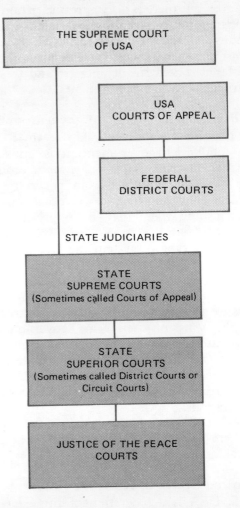

THE LAW COURTS OF THE USA

THE FEDERAL JUDICIARY

THE SUPREME COURT OF USA

USA COURTS OF APPEAL

FEDERAL DISTRICT COURTS

STATE JUDICIARIES

STATE SUPREME COURTS (Sometimes called Courts of Appeal)

STATE SUPERIOR COURTS (Sometimes called District Courts or Circuit Courts)

JUSTICE OF THE PEACE COURTS

ally judged according to whether the result is in the interest of the State.

The chief legal officer of the Soviet Union is the Procurator-General who, according to the Constitution, exercises 'supreme supervisory power to ensure the strict observance of the law'. There are procurators also in each state and locally. All the procurators work entirely within Communist Party policy.

Another branch of Soviet law, which handles many cases, is called State Arbitration. Because there is no private enterprise in the Soviet Union, there is no body of civil

THE SYSTEM OF LAW COURTS OF THE USSR

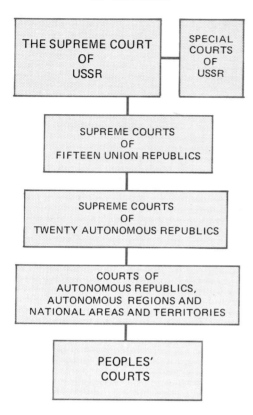

```
┌─────────────────────┐   ┌──────────┐
│  THE SUPREME COURT  │   │ SPECIAL  │
│         OF          │───│ COURTS   │
│        USSR         │   │   OF     │
│                     │   │  USSR    │
└─────────────────────┘   └──────────┘
          │
┌─────────────────────┐
│   SUPREME COURTS    │
│         OF          │
│ FIFTEEN UNION REPUBLICS │
└─────────────────────┘
          │
┌─────────────────────┐
│   SUPREME COURTS    │
│         OF          │
│ TWENTY AUTONOMOUS REPUBLICS │
└─────────────────────┘
          │
┌─────────────────────┐
│     COURTS  OF      │
│ AUTONOMOUS REPUBLICS, │
│ AUTONOMOUS REGIONS AND │
│ NATIONAL AREAS AND TERRITORIES │
└─────────────────────┘
          │
┌─────────────────────┐
│      PEOPLES'       │
│      COURTS         │
└─────────────────────┘
```

SUPERVISION OF LAW IN THE USSR

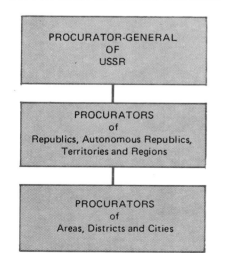

```
┌─────────────────────────────┐
│   PROCURATOR-GENERAL        │
│         OF                  │
│         USSR                │
└─────────────────────────────┘
          │
┌─────────────────────────────┐
│       PROCURATORS           │
│          of                 │
│ Republics, Autonomous Republics, │
│   Territories and Regions   │
└─────────────────────────────┘
          │
┌─────────────────────────────┐
│       PROCURATORS           │
│          of                 │
│  Areas, Districts and Cities │
└─────────────────────────────┘
```

A divorce case being heard in a People's Court in the USSR

law or commercial law, so disputes between State enterprises or factories go to the State Arbitration Courts, whose decision is binding.

There are three kinds of crime in Russia: political, economic and ordinary. A large number of crimes are dealt with as political crimes, for the government seeks to protect itself against any political criticism or opposition. Jack Miller in his book *Life in Russia Today* (Batsford 1969) said: 'In the 1930s the proportion of the adult population arrested or sentenced for alleged political crimes was at least a twentieth and possibly a tenth.'

Alexander Solzhenitsyn in his book *The Gulag Archipelago* (Collins/Fontana 1974), which was suppressed in the USSR and led to his exile, gives an account of the systematic arrest, imprisonment and forced labour from 1918–1956 of millions of people.

It will be understood that an individual's view of the Rule of Law is very different in the USSR or any other country where the law is used for political purposes.

FOR INVESTIGATION AND DISCUSSION

1 Find out in which countries the basic freedoms exist and do not exist.

2 Do you believe that you have more or less freedom in the country where you live than you would have in other countries? Give reasons for your opinions.

3 Why do you think that the system of law in the Soviet Union is so different from that in England or the USA?

4 Discuss or write about your attitude to law if you were living in a country which had a totalitarian government which which you completely disagreed?

5 Try to discover what the legal system is like in at least two other countries which are not mentioned in this section. Seek the help of your school, Public Library or friends.

6 Find out if any countries other than England and the USA have a system such as *Habeas Corpus* to protect people from arrest and imprisonment without charge or trial.

7 Study the newspapers and other journals, and see if you can find any cases where a person has had his freedom threatened, or has been unjustly treated in your opinion. Prepare a short talk on this giving details, and the reasons for your opinion.

8 Try to find an example of the treatment of a person in another country whose freedom has been seriously threatened or curtailed. Prepare a report of the circumstances.

9 What systems of government are there? Find out how laws are made under the different systems. What provision is made in each system for those who wish to change certain laws?

10 What is meant by anarchy? Why have democratic governments sometimes been replaced by dictatorships or military rule?

11 Give examples from other cultures known to you to show how laws and customs of different peoples may differ widely from our own.

12 Should laws be primarily (a) for the good of society as a whole (b) to strengthen the power of government or (c) to protect minorities?

3

THE ENGLISH LEGAL SYSTEM

COMMON LAW	EQUITY depending on Common Law and adding to it	STATUTE LAW

The Law of England and Wales may be divided into Common Law, Equity and Statute Law. In recent times the divisions between Common Law and Equity have become less distinct and closer to one another.

Common Law

English Common Law is also the foundation of the law of the United States of America and that of a number of countries of the Commonwealth. So we can take this as a basis for the understanding of Common Law in those countries too.

To put it simply, Common Law is law which has derived from custom, law of precedent or case law.

Sources of Law

Henry of Bracton, a judge at the time of King Henry III at the end of the thirteenth century, made the ealiest attempt at a systematic treatment of the body of English law. His treatise was based on a collection of cases and later published. Certain other books written many years ago are respected as works of authority. They are not often consulted since there are many changes in laws, but sometimes they are found to be very useful hundreds of years after they were written.

Another book regarded as an authority is the famous *Commentaries* by Sir William Blackstone, an eighteenth-century judge. In this he defined Common Law as:

1. General customs which are the common law
2. Particular customs prevailing in certain districts
3. Laws used in particular courts

There may be local customs in some districts regarding the right to pasture sheep or other animals on common land. The Law will give effect to these customs based on their long use. Another example of law based on custom is that of fencing to prevent animals damaging a neighbour's crops (see p. 9).

Present-day laws regarding cheques and other money matters have arisen from the customs of merchants in their business dealings.

The validity of these customs and usages is determined by the judges, whose judgements are kept and can be referred to when similar cases arise.

These records are the law reports of the cases actually decided. In fact, as the famous English statesman Edmund Burke (1729–1797) said, 'To put an end to reports is to put an end to the law of England.' So this is what we mean by the law of precedent, or case law. A point of law which has been decided before (a precedent), will be used to decide the judgement in a new but similar case. Reference is made to it by giving the names of the people concerned in the case, then the date on which judgement was given. Here are three amusing examples:

Carlill v. Carbolic Smoke Ball Co. (1893)
This case not only affected the law of contract but also advertising. The Carbolic Smoke Ball Co. were makers of a medical preparation called the Carbolic Smoke Ball which they advertised as being capable of preventing colds and influenza if used as directed. Their advertisement in the *Pall Mall Gazette* is reproduced below.

A lady named Carlill bought one of the balls at a chemist's and used it as directed, three times a day, from 20 November 1891 to 17 January 1892, when she caught influenza. She sued the company. Their defence was that there was no contract– their advertisement was just a trade puff. The court, however, ruled that the advertisement constituted an offer, that Mrs Carlill had accepted that offer and therefore a contract had been made. So she received the £100, and the point was established that an advertisement making an offer which is

Carbolic Smoke Ball Co. advertisement which appeared in *The Pall Mall Gazette*

taken up constitutes a contract. It is also a warning to advertisers for it shows how the public may be safeguarded against dishonest statements in advertisements.

McAlister v. Stevenson (1932)

A later example of where the ordinary person can be protected against a business firm comes from Scotland, and concerned negligence.

Stevenson was a maker of ginger beer which was sold in a bottle of dark coloured glass. A friend of McAlister's bought her a bottle of this ginger beer in a café at Paisley. McAlister drank some of it poured out into a tumbler; it was alleged that when her friend proceeded to pour out the rest of the ginger beer bottle into the tumbler a decomposed snail floated out of the bottle. McAlister claimed that as a result of seeing the snail and of having swallowed some of the ginger beer, she became ill, suffering from shock and gastro-enteritis. She brought an action against Stevenson on the grounds that he (a) should have provided a system that would not allow snails to get into his ginger beer bottles (b) should have provided a better system of inspection. The action was at first dismissed, but after appeal McAlister's case was upheld.

This case helped to make the law regarding negligence (lack of care) and the duty of a manufacturer to have proper safeguards, so protecting the public. Negligence is a part of the law of *tort* (see pp. 23 and 24).

Tolley v. J. S. Fry and Sons Ltd. (1931)

Although libel and slander usually mean something to most people, it may not be realised that *defamation*, which is the general legal term, may take many forms.

A famous case is an example of this.

Tolley was a well-known amateur golfer and Frys were a firm of chocolate manufacturers. One of their advertisements showed a cartoon of Tolley playing golf with a

packet of Fry's chocolate sticking out of his pocket. His caddy also was shown with a packet of chocolate. Under the cartoon was a verse:

The caddy to Tolley said, 'Oh Sir,
Good shot, Sir! That ball, see it go, Sir.
My word how it flies
Like a carton of Frys,
They're handy, they're good and priced low, Sir.'

Frys had not got Tolley's permission for this. He sued Frys for libel alleging that readers of the advertisement might think he had agreed to it and received a reward from Frys accordingly, and so damaged his status as an amateur player.

The case was left to the jury who found in favour of Tolley and awarded £1,000 damages. J. S. Fry & Sons Ltd. appealed and the Court of Appeal decided that the damages were too high.

These are cases of special interest, involving decisions of some years ago which have helped to make the laws of *contract* and *tort* today.

Where there is no precedent (no previous judgement), the judge making the decision creates new law by extending existing law to new situations. Thus it may be said that much of Common Law is judge-made law.

21

Equity

This is a branch of law that has grown up over a long period of time, largely to fill in gaps not covered by Common Law. It was mostly connected with laws to do with the ownership of land. Where Common Law did not seem to meet a case fairly, petition could be made to the Chancellor. The old equity court, or Court of Chancery, was described as 'a court of conscience'. Later, by Acts of 1873 and 1875, the Court of Chancery was combined with Common Law Courts to form the Supreme Court.

Equity is really part of the Common Law, but it is sometimes treated separately. Rules of Equity are applied in all divisions of the Court. Where there is conflict between the rules of Law and Equity, the benefit is given to the Equity.

Trusts belong to the law of Equity. It is not easy to define a trust in simple terms, but it is a relationship which arises where property is given to a person or people to take care of (act as trustees) for a particular purpose or for other people. For example, a trustee may be appointed to hold a sum of money or property in trust for a child until the child reaches a certain age. The actions of a trustee are very strictly controlled by law.

Mortgages also come within the law of Equity. A mortgage is when a sum of money is lent on a security, usually of a house or land. (See p. 61.)

Taking out a mortgage

Statute Law

A statute is an Act of Parliament, so statute law is law which is made through Acts which are passed in Parliament. Statutes have been made throughout the centuries and much of what was originally Common Law has been changed by or included in statutes. When an Act is passed, it is said to have been placed upon the Statute Book. As time goes by, more and more of the law becomes Statute Law while Common Law based on custom tends to become less, although judge-made Common Law (that is, case law) continues to increase. Common Law may never override Statute Law. However, statutes cannot anticipate all possible circumstances and they may be extended or interpreted by Case Law. An example is the Sale of Goods Act of 1893. Although this statute still stands, it has been extended and built on as different circumstances have arisen over a period of time. Its interpretation has been subject to considerable discussion.

Constitutional Law

This is the body of Common Law, Statutes, Rules and Conventions which regulates the government of the country. It concerns the position of the Sovereign and the Royal Family, government in all its forms, elections, and most particularly the rights and privileges of ordinary people (see Section 8).

Criminal Law

Criminal Law is distinct from Civil law.

Criminal Law is the branch of public law which relates to criminals—those who commit crimes. What is a crime? A simple, if not completely accurate, definition of a crime is 'an offence against the community at large, as represented by the State and punishable by the State'.

The State, through the elected representatives of the people, decides what is a crime. Anyone who commits a crime (criminal offence) is punished in order to protect the community. Much of Criminal Law is now in statutes, but it still owes much to Common Law.

Civil Law

Civil Law concerns relations and disputes between individuals or groups. The Law will declare judgement for compensation or damages which must be given to the injured party or parties. It will also give instructions that something must be done, or must not be done. Civil Law covers:

contract
tort
domestic relations
trusts
property
industrial relations

In a highly complicated society, rules of conduct are necessary between individuals and groups in their normal daily relations with each other, whether in family life, social life or in business.

A sale of goods constitutes a contract

Contracts are agreements between individuals or groups which have the force of law behind them. The law of contract is a highly developed branch of civil law.

Trespass

A *tort* is a civil wrong—where the Law recognises that wrong has been done which concerns an individual or group and not the community as a whole. It is not a crime. Where the verdict is given that a tort has been committed, damages or compensation are usually awarded and the Court may also rule that the tort must not be committed again, that is that a certain action must cease. Examples of torts are:

trespass
negligence
assault

Assault

23

nuisance

defamation, which includes libel and slander.

Matrimonial law, or the law of domestic relations, includes divorce, separation, maintenance and similar situations.

Nuisance

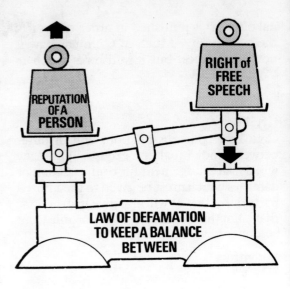

RIGHT of FREE SPEECH

REPUTATION OF A PERSON

LAW OF DEFAMATION TO KEEP A BALANCE BETWEEN

TORT: THE NEIGHBOUR PRINCIPLE

Three main points regarding a tort

1 A duty of care
2 A breach of that duty
3 Damage resulting from that breach.

Duty of care. To whom is that duty owed? Lord Atkin in *McAlister Stevenson* (p. 21) said:
'The rule that you are to love your neighbour becomes, in law, you must not injure your neighbour; and the lawyer's question, Who is my neighbour? receives a restricted reply. You must take reasonable care to avoid acts or omissions which you can reasonably forsee would be likely to injure your neighbour. Who, then, is my neighbour? The answer seems to be—persons who are so closely and directly affected by my act that I ought reasonably to have them in contemplation as being so affected when I am directing my mind to the acts or omissions which are called in question.'
This was the basis for an extension of the law of negligence, and is a good example of a precedent as it was quoted in subsequent cases.

How law is made

Making an Act of Parliament is a long process. The proposal for a new law must be put into legal language by the Parliamentary Counsel's Office. The Bill, as it is then called, is presented to the House of Commons for the First Reading. Sometimes it may go first to the House of Lords. A Second Reading then takes place when the Bill is discussed and debated and goes to the committee stage. It is then discussed in much greater detail, clause by clause, by a Standing Committee or if it is a very important or controversial bill, by the whole House sitting in Committee. If it has been dealt with by a Standing Committee, the Report Stage follows, when the findings of the Committee are reported to the House. Naturally, this is not necessary if the Bill has already been discussed by the whole House. At the Third Reading it is again debated. To pass the Second and Third Readings, voting, or a division, usually takes place. If the vote is in favour of the Bill, the same procedure must take place in the House of Lords (or Commons, if it went first to the House of Lords). If the Bill is passed through both the House of Commons and the House of Lords, it goes to the Queen for the Royal Assent, and the Bill then becomes an Act.

How law is made in Britain the progress of a bill...

1 IDEA for a new law

2 PARLIAMENTARY COUNSELS OFFICE Bill drawn up in legal language

3 FIRST READING Bill introduced by Minister and name announced

4 LAID ON THE TABLE OF THE HOUSE Bill printed and distributed to Members of Parliament and other interested people

5 SECOND READING Bill debated fully in the House. Speeches from all parties

6 COMMITTEE STAGE Committee of whole House for money or controversial Bills. Standing Committee for other Bills. Discussed in detail clause by clause

7 REPORT STAGE No need to report if Committee of whole house Report on work of Standing Committee otherwise

8 THIRD READING Fully debated and vote normally taken

9 TO HOUSE OF LORDS If Bill passes its readings in the House of Commons it goes to the House of Lords

TO HOUSE OF LORDS

10 HOUSE OF LORDS Bill goes through similar procedure to the House of Commons — three readings and Committee stage

11 If Bill passes the House of Lords it goes for the Royal Assent. The House of Lords may not delay a Money Bill but may delay others for about a year

TO THE ROYAL PALACE

12 THE ROYAL ASSENT The Bill goes to the Queen for the Royal Assent. It then becomes Law and the Bill becomes an Act or a Statute

This same process applies to changing an existing law. It takes time to do this, and public opinion is an important factor. It is important for the elected representatives, Members of Parliament, to know what the people they represent think about the matters coming up in Parliament. Sometimes they hold meetings in their constituencies or individual people or groups of people may 'lobby' their MP to let him know their opinion and try to influence him.

When it is necessary to amend laws because of a change in social attitudes or conditions, attempts are made to bring them up to date, though this takes time. Lawyers need to research and study the issues involved. Often many Bills are presented to Parliament at the same time, so some may have to wait. But changes are often made. For instance, the Theft Act of 1968 which has replaced the Larceny Act of 1916 has simplified the law as it applies to theft and to burglary. The Criminal Justice Act of 1972 allows compensation to be paid to a victim by the offender. The Matrimonial Causes Act of 1973 defines more clearly the law about divorce.

Sometimes a bill might be passed very quickly, within a matter of days, usually if this is an emergency. An example is the Prevention of Terrorism Act, 1974, made necessary by bombings in Birmingham and elsewhere in Britain.

The purpose of laws

As we have seen, all societies make rules to regulate conduct. The information given about English Law shows that its purpose is to protect the community from wrongful acts such as crimes, and to regulate the relations between individual and groups so that they are protected from illegal acts. It also ensures the smooth running of society, as far as is possible.

The effect of bombings in Birmingham

Expression of public opinion can often lead to a change in law. Here an MP is being 'lobbied'.

As Ronald Rubinstein says in *John Citizen and the Law*:

If, in fact, everyone respected the rights of every other member of the community, we should not require any rule or law to deal with or punish crime.... Even the disappearance of crime would not, however, relieve the country of its obligations to make laws. We should still require rules to regulate our relations with each other.

FOR INVESTIGATION AND DISCUSSION

1 Do you agree with the above statement? Give arguments for and against, or conduct a debate on: are laws necessary for the smooth running of society?

2 What can be done to bring about more respect for the rights of other people in everyday life? Taking a day in anybody's life, discuss what rights of other people they are likely not to respect?

3 What is meant by Common Law? What is meant by Case Law? Explain each carefully, giving examples of each.

4 What is the difference between a crime and a tort? Give examples of each.

5 Explain how a new law is made in Britain and suggest what groups of people may be concerned with it at each stage.

6 Do you find the legal system of England difficult to understand? Give reasons for your answer.

7 What reforms in English law would you like to see come about?

4

HOW LEGAL SYSTEMS IN BRITAIN WORK

ENGLISH COURTS OF LAW

For many years the pattern of English Law Courts was set by the County Courts Act of 1846, and the Judicature and other Acts of 1873 and 1875.

From then until 1972 there was a system of Petty Sessions, Quarter Sessions and Assizes, with the divisions of the High Court and the County Court. Considerable changes were made by the Courts Act of 1971, which came into force on 1 January 1972. This Act left some of the existing courts as they were. The system is now as follows:

Magistrates Courts (Petty Sessions)

These are also known as Police Courts. They are mainly concerned with criminal law and deal with the less serious cases, such as motoring offences and minor cases of theft. They are also called courts of 'First Instance', as they carry out the preliminary investigation of more serious criminal offences which will be tried in a higher court. These are known as committal proceedings. Magistrates Courts are also concerned with licensing laws and have a limited civil jurisdiction, mainly in family cases such as actions for separation and maintenance. These are the courts, together with County Courts, which most affect ordinary people.

The Magistrates are Justices of the Peace (JPs), members of the public who do not necessarily have any legal training, but who normally have a clerk who is a trained lawyer to advise them on points of law and procedure. JPs perform their duties voluntarily and without payment. There must be at least two JPs sitting together to constitute a Court and there are usually more. In a very busy area, a stipendiary or full-time magistrate may be appointed who must be a trained lawyer.

Metropolitan Magistrates Courts

Because London is such a huge, crowded city, with a very large population, it is not surprising that the amount of work for the lower courts is enormous. Therefore, the system of Petty Sessions courts with voluntary magistrates just would not work.

For this reason London has its own system of Metropolitan Magistrates Courts which perform roughly the same functions as the courts of Petty Session. Each is staffed by stipendary magistrates who sit alone and possess the powers of two Justices of the Peace sitting together in Petty Sessions.

Juvenile Courts

These are part of the Magistrates Courts. The magistrates, who are both men and women, are carefully selected and have a special interest in children and young

28

Magistrates' Court in session. The four magistrates are seen sitting on the bench.

Inside a Juvenile Court. The Court Usher is administering the Oath to the witness. Also in the photograph are the Clerk of the Court, a Counsel and a Social Worker.

offenders. An attempt is made to make the proceedings less formal than in the other Magistrates Courts and to help the young offenders not to repeat their offences.

County Courts

County Courts are responsible for most of the cases under civil law in England. They deal with contract, tort, property, wills, debts and bankruptcy. Four-fifths of divorce cases are decided in the County Courts. The procedure in a County Court is more simple than that in the High Court. Some straightforward and undefended cases may be decided by the Court Registrar without appearing in the Court proper at all. The County Courts are staffed by judges, who must be barristers of at least seven years' standing. The Registrars must be experienced solicitors.

A young French Magistrate

29

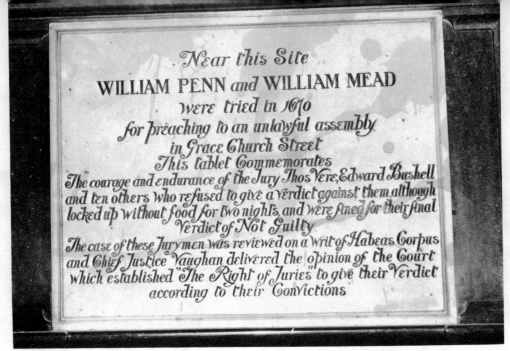

Near this Site...

WILLIAM PENN and WILLIAM MEAD
were tried in 1670
for preaching to an unlawful assembly
in Grace Church Street
This tablet Commemorates
The courage and endurance of the Jury Thos Vere, Edward Bushell
and ten others who refused to give a verdict against them, although
locked up without food for two nights, and were fined for their final
Verdict of Not Guilty
The case of these Jurymen was reviewed on a Writ of Habeas Corpus
and Chief Justice Vaughan delivered the opinion of the Court
which established "The Right of Juries" to give their Verdict
according to their Convictions

This tablet at the Old Bailey commemorates the precedent establishing the 'Right of Juries'

Since the Courts Act of 1971, Crown Court Judges are also County Court Judges and County Court Judges may also sit in Crown Courts. Circuit Judges are appointed to sit in Crown Courts and County Courts and must be barristers of at least ten years' standing or Recorders of five years' standing.

Crown Courts

The Courts Act of 1971 abolished both Courts of Quarter Session and Assize Courts and replaced them with a system of Crown Courts. Crown Courts are superior courts of record and are a part of the Supreme Court. When the Crown Court sits in the City of London it is known as the Central Criminal Court, popularly called the Old Bailey.

Crown Courts deal with all the more serious criminal cases and have considerable civil jurisdiction, which was formerly a part of the proceedings of the High Court.

Crown Courts also act as appeal courts from Petty Sessions courts and Metropolitan Magistrates Courts and when this is so

the judge of the Crown Court sits with not less than two nor more than four Justices of the Peace.

Crown Courts may be staffed by High Court Judges, Circuit Judges or Recorders, who are practising lawyers. Recorders serve as part-time judges.

The High Court

The High Court consists of the Queen's Bench Division, the Chancery Division and the Family Division.

The Queen's Bench Division

This originated in the old King's court with the King's judges which was set up in the Middle Ages. It has both criminal and civil jurisdiction, although it is concerned only with special criminal cases such as treason or crimes committed by a public official out of England. As far as civil actions are concerned it hears cases of many different kinds and deals with almost all types of civil case. There are two specialised courts—the Commercial Court and the Admiralty Court.

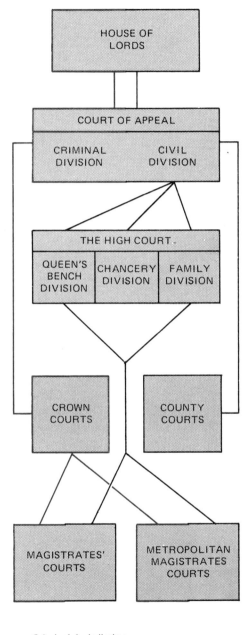

THE COURTS OF LAW
SINCE THE COURTS ACT, 1971

HOUSE OF
LORDS

COURT OF APPEAL

CRIMINAL
DIVISION

CIVIL
DIVISION

THE HIGH COURT.

QUEEN'S
BENCH
DIVISION

CHANCERY
DIVISION

FAMILY
DIVISION

CROWN
COURTS

COUNTY
COURTS

MAGISTRATES'
COURTS

METROPOLITAN
MAGISTRATES
COURTS

Criminal Jurisdiction ———————

Civil Jurisdiction ———————

The Chancery Division

This originated in the old court of Chancery, or Lord Chancellor's Court, from which grew up the law of Equity. Although the Chancery Division today deals with many different kinds of cases, it is concerned only with Civil Law, hears cases without a jury, and still tends to specialise in many Equity matters, particularly estates, partnerships, mortgages, trusts, contracts and guardianship. In theory, the Lord Chancellor is still President of the Division with the Master of the Rolls as his deputy, but, in practice, the Lord Chancellor never sits and the Master of the Rolls is now permanently in the Court of Appeal.

The Family Division

Since the Administration of Justice Act of 1970 the Divorce and Probate sections have been combined as the Family Division. It deals with matrimonial cases and wills.

The Court of Appeal

This is in two divisions, Civil and Criminal. They hear cases on appeals from the civil and criminal sides of the Crown Courts and the High Court. The Lord Chief Justice of England is normally President of the Court of Appeal, Criminal Division. The Master of the Rolls (see pp. 32, 33) normally presides over the Court of Appeal (Civil Division).

The House of Lords

The House of Lords is the final court of appeal. Appeals may be made to it by permission of the Court of Appeal. If permission is not granted application may be made to the Appeal Committee of the House of Lords. When the House of Lords sits as an appeal court its judges are drawn from the Lord Chancellor, any ex-Lord Chancellor, members of the House of Lords who were judges, and the Lords of Appeal.

31

Judges in their formal robes

Minister. He ranks immediately after the Lord Chief Justice and is the virtual head of the Court of Appeal. He is called the Master of the Rolls because he is responsible for all the records at the Public Record Office. He is also head of the solicitor branch of the legal profession.

Master of the Rolls

The Judges

The Lord Chancellor is the senior judge. His appointment is political as well as judicial. He is appointed by the Queen on the advice of the Prime Minister and is a member of the Cabinet. He presides over the House of Lords in its normal sittings, as well as judicial sittings. He is also the Leader of the Government in the House of Lords. He advises on the appointment of judges.

The Lord Chief Justice of England is appointed by the Queen on the advice of the Prime Minister. He is responsible for the administration of the courts and is particularly concerned with criminal law.

The Master of the Rolls is also appointed by the Queen on the advice of the Prime

The Lord Justices are senior judges and usually sit in the Court of Appeal although they may be requested to sit in any division of the High Court.

The Puisne Judges are so-called because the French word *puisne* like the word 'puny' means 'lesser' or 'weaker'; they are the most junior of the High Court judges. They are the judges who sit in the divisions of the High Court although for some serious cases they may also sit in Crown Courts.

Since the Courts Act of 1971 Circuit Judges are appointed as judges of Crown Courts or County Courts.

Recorders are part-time judges of the Crown Courts. They must be barristers or solicitors of at least ten years' standing.

The Lord Chancellor may direct circuit judges or recorders to sit as judges of the High Court if necessary.

Until recently all judges were appointed from the ranks of barristers but it is now possible for a solicitor to become a judge.

A Crown Court. (From the Crown Court Series— Granada TV.)

THE LEGAL PROFESSION

The Legal Profession, apart from judges, is divided into two main parts, barristers and solicitors. This is an unusual distinction which exists only in England and Wales and some Commonwealth countries. In almost all other countries there is no distinction between the functions of legal profession. Legal executives are a comparatively new branch of the legal profession. Their function is described later.

Barristers

The term barrister or, more correctly, barrister-at-law is applied to persons who have been called to the Bar by one of the four Inns of Court, and they are the senior branch of the legal profession. No person can practise as a barrister unless he is a member of one of these Inns.

The Inns of Court, known as the Inner Temple, the Middle Temple, Lincoln's Inn and Gray's Inn, are independent of State control although subject to inspection by the judges. They are governed by their senior members, known as Masters of the Bench, or Benchers, who are responsible for the education, discipline and admission of barristers. They can exercise their discipline in the last resort by disbarring a member, that is, by preventing him from acting as a barrister. A general control over the whole profession of barristers is exercised by the General Council of the Bar, and the education and examination of intending barristers is carried on by the Council for Legal Education.

Barristers are experts who usually specialise in a fairly narrow field of law. They often give advice on specialist points of law to the solicitor's lay client. They also act as advocates.

Barristers are sometimes called counsel. They have a right of audience, in some cases shared with solicitors, in all courts of law, but in the higher courts, only they have the right of audience. That is to say, they may appear as counsel for the plaintiff or the prosecution or defence in any law case, civil or criminal.

A person who needs counsel may not approach a barrister directly, but only through a solicitor.

There are two grades of barrister. The senior grade is known as Queen's Counsel (QCs), sometimes called 'silks' because they wear silk gowns. They sit within the bar at the Law Courts. The other grade is known as juniors. A Queen's Counsel may not appear in court, except a County Court, without a junior.

33

Lincoln's Inn showing the Library on the left and Barristers' Chambers on the right

Solicitors

Solicitors are the lawyers with whom the public most come into contact. A solicitor shares with a barrister the right of audience in certain courts of law and often appears for the defence or the plaintiff or the prosecution. His main function, however, is to advise clients as to the law in all the many complicated situations of modern life, and to deal with the legal aspects of house-purchase and sale, estates, wills, contracts, mortgages, torts and many other matters which come under the heading of civil law as well as advice in criminal cases. This advice often means the retaining and briefing of a barrister.

The governing body of the solicitor's profession, responsible for education, examination, discipline and admission of solicitors, is the Law Society. If a solicitor is guilty of misconduct, he may be struck off the roll and therefore be prevented from practising.

Legal executives

Legal executives used to be known as solicitors' clerks. Solicitors' clerks, particularly managing clerks, build up a great wealth of experience and knowledge. They now have special qualifications by examination, as with other branches of the profession, and can be Associates or Fellows of the Institute of Legal Executives. These qualifications are recognised and entitle the legal executive to carry on some of the work originally done by solicitors as well as much of the general administration and management of solicitors' offices.

a. Clients consult their solicitor on a legal point

b. Solicitors often have to take instructions from prisoners in custody before appearing in Court on their behalf

c. Solicitors may take cases in Magistrates Courts

d. Solicitors appear as advocates in the County Courts. Here a woman solicitor is conducting a Personal Injury Claim.

The solicitor ensures that his client's rights are enforced—this farmer has land which is needed for the extension of a motorway. In addition to acting for clients in private practice, a solicitor may also act as a legal adviser in a firm, in local government, or in the Civil Service.

HOW CASES ARE DEALT WITH

Civil actions

Civil actions begin with either a writ or a summons. In the High Court, it is more usually a writ, that is a royal command for the defendant to appear within fourteen days of the writ being served. The person who begins the action is known as the plaintiff and the other party is known as the defendant.

The counsel for the plaintiff opens the case by calling the witnesses and evidence he considers necessary. Witnesses may be cross-examined by the defence. The counsel for the defence then opens the defence case, again calling witnesses and producing evidence. They, too, may be cross-examined. Both counsel have a right to make final speeches after the evidence has been given.

Civil cases are almost always tried by judges alone; more rarely by judge and jury.

36

THE NORMAL COURSE OF EVENTS IN A CIVIL DISPUTE

> The allegation

> Attempt by the parties and their legal advisers to settle the dispute without resort to the courts.

> Issue and service of the writ.

> Exchange of the pleadings.

TRIAL
(normal course of the Trial)

1 Opening speech by plaintiff's counsel.
2 Plaintiff's witnesses examined in chief by plaintiffs counsel and cross-examined by defendant counsel.
3 Opening speech by defence counsel.
4 Defendant witnesses examined in chief and cross-examined.
5 Defence counsel's final address.
6 Plaintiff's counsel's final address.
7 The judgement is delivered. The judge frequently states how he comes to his decision. If plaintiff wins a remedy is given.

> Enforcement of the remedy.

Criminal action

There are two main procedures for trying criminal offences. The first is on indictment, or a written charge, which is used for the more serious offences and which means that the accused will be tried in a higher court. The second is where the accused may be tried summarily at a Magistrates Court. In both cases, the accused must be charged and a summons is normally issued.

Let us take the second example first: a person (Jones) is accused of a comparatively minor offence. He will be charged and summoned to appear at a Magistrates Court. In certain cases the accused has a right to be tried by jury and the magistrates must explain this to him. Jones may decide to be tried by jury, when his case must be passed on to a Crown Court. However, he may, if he wish, decide to be tried summarily, that is, at once by the Magistrates Court. In many cases, however, the accused has no right to a jury trial where the offence is very trivial. The accused may be represented by a solicitor or by counsel, that is, a barrister.

In the case of an indictable offence, the case will first be considered by a Magistrates Court sitting as a 'court of the first instance'. The task of the court is to decide whether there is a *prima facie* case, which means that at first sight there appears to be sufficient evidence. This is known as the committal stage. If they decide that this is so then the accused is remanded, either in custody or on bail, for a higher court, usually a Crown Court.

Bail. In certain cases bail may be applied for when the accused is awaiting trial. If granted, this means that the accused is allowed to go free instead of being kept in custody on the promise that he will appear in court when summoned. This promise is backed up by the security of a sum of money which has to be paid if he fails to appear and may be guaranteed and paid by the accused or a friend or relative.

THE STAGES OF TRIAL ON INDICTMENT AT THE CROWN COURT

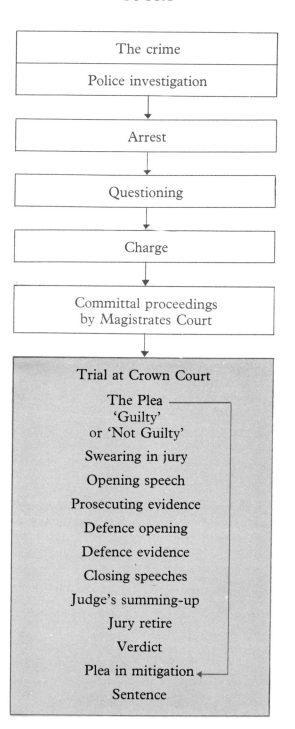

- The crime
- Police investigation
- Arrest
- Questioning
- Charge
- Committal proceedings by Magistrates Court
- Trial at Crown Court
  - The Plea — 'Guilty' or 'Not Guilty'
  - Swearing in jury
  - Opening speech
  - Prosecuting evidence
  - Defence opening
  - Defence evidence
  - Closing speeches
  - Judge's summing-up
  - Jury retire
  - Verdict
  - Plea in mitigation
  - Sentence

At the Crown Court, the accused will normally be represented by counsel. The prosecuting barrister will present his case, calling such witnesses and producing such evidence as is considered necessary. The defence may cross-examine. The defence barrister will then present his case, again producing witnesses and evidence which will also be subject to cross-examination. Both prosecution and defence will make closing speeches. The jury will listen to the evidence and to the judge's summing-up. It should be remembered that it is the duty of the judge to rule on matters of law and the jury to make up its mind on matters of fact. Also the principle of English Law should be remembered—*an accused person is considered to be innocent until he is proved guilty*.

When the jury has given its verdict, the counsel for defence may make a plea in mitigation, the judge will pass sentence if the verdict is 'guilty' and dismiss the charge if it is 'not guilty'.

A great deal of trouble is taken to ensure that only the guilty are sentenced. The prosecution must prove its case beyond reasonable doubt and by admissible evidence, not assumptions.

In both civil and criminal cases legal aid (see p. 64) may be claimed and there is a right of appeal.

Adversary and inquisitional systems

The mode of trial in England is known as the adversary system because the judge holds an impartial central position whilst the two sides contest to establish their respective cases. On the Continent the normal system is inquisitory, with the judge playing a more active part, leading the investigation into the issues. The main example of the inquisitorial approach in England is the Coroner's Court which enquires into reasons for the death of a person, that is, holds an inquest when the circumstances are suspicious.

Juries

Every man or woman who is not less than 18 and not over 65 is liable to be asked to sit on a jury, unless they are ineligible, disqualified or can claim exemption.

Among those who are ineligible are:

judges, including JP's,
people concerned with the administration of justice, such as the police and prison officers
members of the clergy
people who are mentally ill.

Included in those who are disqualified are:

people who have been sentenced to terms of imprisonment of five years or more
people who in the last ten years have been sentenced to imprisonment for three months or have been detained in a Borstal Institution.

Those who may claim exemption include:

MP's
Members of the Armed Forces
doctors
chemists
dentists
veterinary surgeons
and a number of others whose jobs make it difficult to attend a case that may last a number of weeks
people who have served on a jury during the previous two years.

Before the jurors are sworn in, either side may challenge any juror on the grounds of his personality or illegibility. The Defence may reject any juror from serving without giving any reason.

Those called for jury service may be paid travelling and subsistence allowances and compensation for loss of earnings.

A jury consists of twelve members and appoints one of its members as foreman. The foreman acts as chairman while the jury is discussing the case and acts as spokesman for the jury in court.

A jury is responsible for listening to the

evidence and deciding the case on the facts.

Since the Criminal Justice Act of 1967 a jury's verdict in criminal proceedings need not be unanimous, that is to say, a majority verdict is allowed.

If ten of the jury cannot agree on a verdict, there will be a re-trial.

Many cases are settled out of court, in fact most lawyers try to arrange an agreement between the two parties. Sometimes in a civil action both parties may be partly in the wrong. When a case is being heard in court, evidence may be given which shows this to be so. The legal advisers may consult with their clients and this may result in a compromise, each side paying their own costs. A lawyer may also advise his client that although the action may be tried in a High Court after appeal, the case is likely to go against him, so he may advise his client to settle.

CASE STUDY OF CRIMINAL ACTION

Jenkins, aged 22, is walking through a car park when he sees an unattended red Austin motor car with keys carelessly left in the ignition. He immediately decides to take the car and drive it away. He obtains false number plates and a log book from criminal

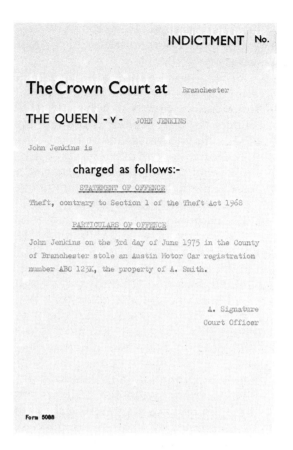

INDICTMENT No.

The Crown Court at Branchester

THE QUEEN - v - JOHN JENKINS

John Jenkins is

charged as follows:-

STATEMENT OF OFFENCE

Theft, contrary to Section 1 of the Theft Act 1968

PARTICULARS OF OFFENCE

John Jenkins on the 3rd day of June 1975 in the County of Branchester stole an Austin Motor Car registration number ABC 123K, the property of A. Smith.

A. Signature
Court Officer

Form 5088

acquaintances and takes it to 'The Good Value Garage' to see if they would like to purchase it. The manager takes the car for a trial drive but whilst doing so he fails to stop at a red traffic light and is brought to a halt by the observant PC Nixon and Sgt Sharpe. Whilst taking notes of the incident Sgt Sharpe recalls that a similar car was recently reported stolen. After satisfying themselves that it is the stolen car they return with the manager to the Garage. The police officers ask Jenkins to accompany them to the Police Station and he agrees.

The police caution Jenkins, question him about the offence and his movements that day. When they have sufficient information he is charged with theft by a senior police officer. Jenkins applies for and is granted legal aid and therefore has the services of

39

a solicitor and counsel. He is committed by the Magistrates Court for trial at the Crown Court.

The trial at the Crown Court

When the judge is ready to begin the clerk announces the case. Jenkins is brought up from the cells and stands in the dock. The clerk reads the indictment to him and asks if he understands it. (An indictment is a document giving formal information relevant to the trial, naming the offence charged together with the main details.) Jenkins is then asked whether he pleads 'Guilty'. He pleads 'Not guilty'.

The jurors are called into the court and individually sworn in. They sit together in reserved seats and are instructed that they must not discuss the case with anyone else. They are told the charge laid against the accused and that he has pleaded 'Not guilty'.

The prosecution counsel rises and delivers an opening speech in which he outlines to the Court the main facts of the case and the evidence by which he proposes to show that the offence was committed by Jenkins. The prosecution counsel is the representative of the Crown and his role is to put the evidence before the Court. It is not his task to secure a conviction. He then calls the evidence. The witnesses must stay out of the courtroom until it is their turn to give evidence. They are sworn in and are first asked questions by the prosecution counsel and are then cross-examined by the defence counsel. The car owner is first called. He identifies the car as his and states that it was taken on the particular date from the car park without his permission. The next witness is the car park attendant who identifies Jenkins as being in the car park and driving away a red car. The garage manager is called to say that Jenkins offered to sell him the car. The police officers also describe their part in the events. The number plates and log book will also be proved to be false.

At the close of the case for the Prosecution the defence counsel calls Jenkins (who has chosen to give evidence on oath; he could have given it without the oath, or kept silent). He states falsely that he was in a neighbouring town at the time he was alleged to be in the car park. He later bought the car from a man in the 'Two Lions' Public House but that unfortunately the man has disappeared. He is not able to produce an alibi—that is someone who saw him in the Public House. He is then cross-examined by the prosecution.

Prosecution and defence counsels then make closing speeches.

The judge then commences his summing up. He instructs a jury that it is for the prosecution to prove beyond doubt that Jenkins is guilty and that if they are not sure that they must acquit him. He then reviews the evidence and directs their minds to the main points. He tells them what the law is but leaves all decisions of fact to them. He asks them to reach a unanimous verdict.

The jury return to the Jury Room and consider the evidence. It may only be imagined how the jury arrive at their conclusion as members of the jury are forbidden to discuss this matter afterwards. This rule is for their own protection.

When the jury have reached a verdict they come back into the Court. They are asked if they have arrived at a unanimous verdict and if they have whether they find the accused 'Guilty' or 'Not guilty' of the offence charged. The foreman of the jury announces that they find Jenkins guilty.

The police then give details of Jenkins' Criminal Record. This shows that he has a history of crime and in particular theft. This is the first time that the Court is informed of his criminal past and therefore his trial was not prejudiced by his record.

The defence counsel addresses the Court and delivers a plea in mitigation in which he outlines facts which may explain or excuse Jenkins' behaviour. The judge is also helped by a Social Inquiry Report.

The judge then decides on the sentence bearing in mind the nature of the offence, the criminal record, the plea in mitigation and the Social Inquiry Report.

THE SCOTTISH LEGAL SYSTEM

The Parliaments of England and Scotland were joined by the Act of Union in 1707. Though the two kingdoms were united, both already had their own legal systems and these differences were maintained. So today English and Scottish courts have different jurisdiction, different procedures, and apply different laws.

There are a number of laws that apply equally to Scotland, England and Wales, as the great majority of Statutes enacted by Parliament apply to the whole of the United Kingdom, for example, the Finance Acts dealing with income tax and capital gains tax.

However, the basis of Scots Law is quite different from that of English Law. It is founded on Roman Law which is the basis of many European legal systems. This is because of the strong political links between Scotland and France in the fifteenth century. As a result of this, many Scots studied in the Continental universities and brought back a knowledge of Roman Law. In addition, the Church Courts flourished in Scotland until the Reformation. The final appeal from these courts was to the Pope at the Papal Court at Rome and this also explains the influence of civil law.

As a result of these historical factors, much Scottish Law is quite separate from English Law. The greatest differences are to be found in the law of contract and the laws regulating inheritance. In Conveyancing (the disposing or transferring of land and buildings) Scots Law is entirely separate as it is based on the old 'Feudal System'. Also there is very little leasehold property in Scotland.

Interior of Parliament House, home of the Court of Sessions, the Supreme Court of Scotland

THE SCOTTISH COURTS
Civil Courts

The principal civil court is the Court of Session. It consists of the Inner House and the Outer House.

The Inner House is divided into two divisions, one presided over by the Lord President and the other by the Lord Justice Clerk. These hear appeals from the Outer House and the Sheriff Courts. In the Outer House the judges, who are called Lords of Session, sit alone or occasionally with a jury.

Much of the civil litigation is dealt with by the Sheriff Courts, which have extensive civil jurisdiction but they may not hear certain cases, in particular divorce cases.

There is normally a right of appeal on points of law from the Inner House of the Court of Session to the House of Lords. At least one member of the Lords of Appeal in Ordinary is a former Scottish lawyer. The Judicial Committee of the House of Lords will give its judgement based on Scottish Law. The decision may affect

41

English Law. The case of *McAlister v. Stevenson* (see p. 21) was settled on an appeal from the Court of Session and became a basis for the extension of liability for negligence in English law.

Criminal courts

The principal criminal court is the High Court of Justiciary, which has exclusive jurisdiction over the more serious criminal offences. Its judges are those who sit in the Court of Session. It may also sit as an appeal court and when it is so sitting its decisions are final as there is no appeal to the House of Lords in criminal cases.

Court procedure

Scotland is divided into six sheriffdoms and each is presided over by a full-time Sheriff-Principal appointed by the Crown. Each Sheriff-Principal has under him a number of Sheriffs who hold court in the principal towns of the sheriffdom.

Minor criminal offences, formerly heard in the J.P. or Burgh Police Courts, are now heard in 'District Courts' over which a stipendiary magistrate or one or more Justices of the Peace preside.

Evidence

The law of evidence is different from that of England. In jury trials in both criminal and civil trials, majority verdicts have always been acceptable. There are fifteen members of a Scottish jury and a majority of one is sufficient. In criminal cases the jury have a choice of three verdicts: 'Not guilty', 'Guilty', and 'Not proven'.

Legal profession

The legal profession of Scotland closely resembles that of England. The equivalent of the English solicitor is also normally called a solicitor, though in Aberdeen he is called an Advocate and in Glasgow is often called a Writer.

The equivalent of the English barrister is called an Advocate and after several years' practice he or she may become a Queen's Counsel.

FOR INVESTIGATION AND DISCUSSION

1 Give an account of the functions performed by the different types of court in England and Wales.
2 A has been charged with the theft of a motorbike belonging to B. Tell the story of what happens from A's arrest to his being found innocent or guilty.
3 Find out about the local courts in your area. You might find an account of a case at one of them in your local paper.
4 Try to arrange a visit to one of your local courts. Write down your impressions and reactions to what you see and hear, and the different types of cases.
5 Find out in detail about the work of a solicitor, a barrister, a magistrate, a judge and a legal executive. You may be able to do this by personal interview.
6 If you were to be tried for assault, discuss whether you would rather be tried by judge sitting alone or by judge and jury.
7 Discuss the system of trial by jury and whether you agree with the lists of those who are ineligible or exempt.
8 If possible, find out how a case is tried in another country from your own and note the differences that strike you in how it is conducted.

5
LAW ENFORCEMENT

Violent crime has become such a problem in Munich, Western Germany, that the police wear iron masks and bullet-proof vests as protection when dealing with criminals who may be armed and dangerous.

The Police

It is the duty of governments, democratically elected or otherwise, to make laws; the courts interpret them and administer them; but it is the police on whom the main responsibility falls for law enforcement.

In some countries the army is called in to assist the police in keeping law and order. In the USA, for example, National Guardsmen, the American equivalent of British Territorial Volunteers, are often mobilised to help the police. This is more easily and quickly done because the National Guard is under the direct control of the governor of each state.

In most countries the police are armed, usually with a pistol; in some the police are a semi-military force with automatic weapons and armoured cars; and in other countries there are specially organised riot police who are more heavily armed than the others.

Soldiers have rarely been used to help the police in Britain. They were used during the General Strike of 1926 and in more recent times in the unusual and tragic situation in Northern Ireland.

In Britain there are no state police—the police force is not nationally but locally controlled—and no secret police such as exist in some other countries.

Sir Robert Mark, Commissioner of the Metropolitan Police, summed up the situation in these words:

'The police here (Britain) have never been, as in other countries, an executive arm of government. We are not, as is the case in many countries, subject to orders from central or local government, from ministers or officials.... We are accountable for our actions to the law itself, both criminal and civil, to local police authorities, to the central government and ultimately to public opinion.

'A chief officer of police can be sued for damages in respect of the action of an unidentified junior.'

This position of the British police, which involves local general control but central government supervision is almost unique. They have built up a reputation for fairness

43

and for handling all kinds of situations, including civil disturbances, with the minimum of force and the maximum of patience. Traditionally, British police have always been unarmed, but violence in today's society has now led to a change of policy. Policemen patrolling airports are armed and it was suggested that they should openly wear guns, as a result of terrorism at airports and the hi-jacking of planes in 1974. The Police Federation are very much against guns being worn outside the uniforms as they want to keep to their tradition and they say that in the USA and on the Continent, where they are worn on the outside, guns have not proved an effective deterrent.

A unit set up to provide security on a 24-hour basis for foreign embassies and diplomats (Scotland Yard's Diplomatic Protection Group) carry guns permanently, and so do some units of the Yard's Special Patrol Group.

In 1975 the Bomb Squad at the Yard was increased in number. Members are trained in the use of fire-arms and the Squad learnt specialist methods of combatting all forms of urban guerrilla terrorism.

The organisation of the Police in Britain

To many people, whose image of the police is based upon television, the police consists of Scotland Yard who provide the skilled, intelligent detective, and the local police forces.

In fact, New Scotland Yard, to give it its correct title, is the headquarters of the Metropolitan Police. The Metropolitan Police Force covers the area of Greater London, with the exception of the City of London, but its Criminal Investigation Department is often called in to assist provincial police forces.

The Metropolitan Police is under the direction of a Commissioner, with a Deputy Commissioner and several Assistant Commissioners. It is divided into departments concerned with Administration and

Policeman advising two citizens

Operations, Traffic, Criminal Investigation, Personnel and Training, Public Relations and others under the general heading of Administration and Finance. Each department is under an Assistant Commissioner or a Director. The strength of the Metropolitan Police is approximately 21,000.

The City of London Police is under its own Commissioner and is concerned with the area covered by the old city of London. It is about 850 strong.

Local police forces in the past were often quite small. The Police Act of 1964 grouped police forces together. Some purely local forces were replaced by larger forces responsible for much larger areas such as the West Midlands Police or the Thames Valley Police. The police forces were now removed from the authority of local councils. The Local Government Act of 1972 has in some respects brought the police forces and the local authorities closer together again because the new local government areas are similar in size to some of the police force areas.

44

A provincial force is commanded by a Chief Constable who has a Deputy Chief Constable and sometimes several Assistant Chief Constables to assist him. Each provincial police force has its own departments similar to those of the Metropolitan Police.

The Police Act of 1964 set up Police Authorities on which are represented the Local Government Authorities. They are responsible for the police forces under them. The Chief Constables of the police forces concerned are responsible for their direction and control. The final responsibility lies with the Home Secretary.

Regional Crime Squads have recently been formed, staffed by officers drawn from several police forces and responsible for dealing with more serious crimes in the area by professional criminals, for example the passing of forged cheques. Apart from providing a highly skilled force that can take joint action in such cases, officers get the opportunity to gain experience which they might not otherwise have in their own forces.

The role of the police

It can generally be said that most people want to have a peaceful existence, with the minimum danger of interference with them or their property. Only a minority resent the maintenance of law and order.

A policeman may be regarded as a 'peace officer' rather than a 'law officer'. Little of his time is actually spent in arresting offenders. Far more is spent in 'keeping the peace' by patrolling his beat and answering calls for assistance. Schemes have been introduced in some parts of Britain so that young people have a chance to know their police force and the variety of work it does. Two such schemes are the Liaison Scheme, where there are regular visits to schools and the Volunteer Cadet Scheme, where young people actually take part in some police activities.

However, some groups can only see the

Police patrolling in London

police in their role as law enforcers. For instance, protesters often resent the police. As T. A. Critchley says in *The Police We Deserve*, 'Protesters against the established order are very ready to see the police as the very thing Peel set out to avoid—the strong arm of the State, defending privilege and the establishment.'

Clashes between demonstrators and police have sometimes led to accusations of violence and brutality from both sides. Somtimes complaints against the police come from immigrant communities: they may feel that their interests are not being

A Peeler arresting a handkerchief stealer. Early policemen were named after Sir Robert Peel, founder of the Police Force.

45

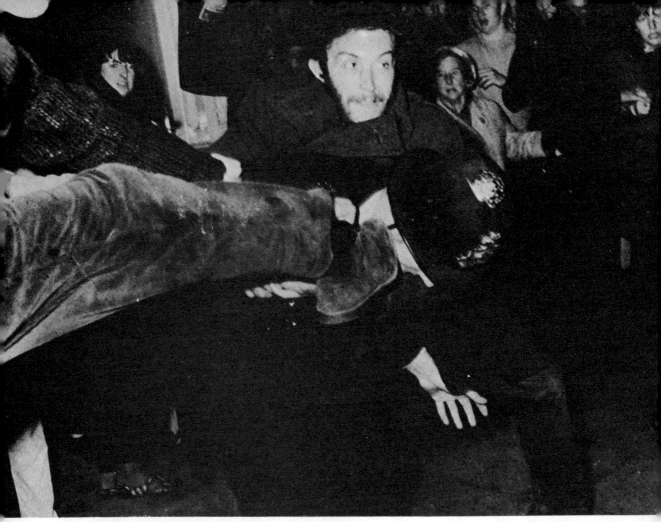

Top: Policeman being attacked during a demonstration
Bottom: Policemen trying to prevent someone from throwing himself over the balcony

protected because so few policemen come from among the immigrant communities and misunderstandings can arise, particularly with the immigrant's unfamiliarity with the law and the policeman's unfamiliarity with the immigrant's language. Attempts to recruit from among these communities and the learning of foreign languages, such as Hindi and Urdu are both ways of solving these problems, which are being adopted.

The Police College, Bramshill

International aspects

The College is the national Police College for the police forces of England and Wales and accepts students from other forces in the United Kingdom. Scotland has its own Police College. Bramshill College has also acquired an international status because of the large numbers of students who come from all parts of the world. The great majority are from Commonwealth countries (both the independent countries and the few remaining dependent territories), but some are from the USA and others from Europe. The College maintains special relationships with police training establishments all over the world and sometimes exchanges staff with them for training purposes.

The College's advice is frequently sought by high police authorities in many countries.

The many overseas officers now in the middle and higher ranks of their forces have done much to help their UK colleagues to see their role in a world context, while they themselves have gained fresh ideas and techniques.

The College provides a chance to get away from day-to-day claims of daily work and to consider wider issues. Officers returning to their duties have a deeper insight into society and so are better able to tackle the problems of community relations.

The College is a focal point for police from all over the world and provides an opportunity for the discussion of society's problems. Its training is very much a preparation for the future.

Police in other countries

Co-operation between the police of different countries has grown in importance as

A scale model of the city of Nairobi is used to instruct police in traffic control there

Records of 930,000 criminals are classified and kept at Interpol

the professional criminal has made use of speedy transport systems to move quickly between countries. The organisation known as INTERPOL (International Police) has had some notable successes, particularly in breaking international drug syndicates. The organisation of the police varies considerably from country to country.

The police in the United States of America are largely locally controlled with little or no direction from the central government. There is no inspectorate of police in America as there is in Britain. Indeed there has been no programme of amalgamation in America with the result that there are over 40,000 police departments for some 175 million people varying in size from that of New York with about 33,000

police to some small departments with about a dozen men or less. The police carry firearms. By the end of 1974 the number of USA police killed on active duty had reached 130.

As a reserve the American police have the National Guard, which has been described as a military force, directly under each State governor. The central government has the Federal Bureau of Investigation, or FBI as it is generally known, which is concerned with the investigation of federal crimes.

In France police are controlled by the central government, the Police Nationale by the Ministry of the Interior and the Gendarmerie Nationale by the Ministry of Defence. All the French police are armed and have considerable reserve forces for emergency use. The Police Nationale have Republican Security Companies (CRS) and the Gendarmerie Nationale have the Gendarmerie Mobile. The association of the police with the use of force often arouses public opinion against the police as in the Paris student riots in 1968.

Secret Police

In totalitarian countries, apart from armed semi-military police forces, controlled by the central government and usually used by it as a political weapon, there are almost always secret police. Because of the nature of their work is secret, one cannot always be sure how accurate information about various secret police forces really is. It is often revealed years after an event has taken place. We can be sure that the secret agent differs from that of the James Bond image. Recent writings by the Russian writer, Solzhenitsyn give vivid descriptions of the role and workings of the KGB in Russian society.

In America the Central Intelligence Agency (CIA) functions almost as a State Department in its own right, with its own policy and overseas representatives. It works in the interests of American politics and economy and constantly works against the forces of communism and counter-espionage.

In Britain, New Scotland Yard has a Special Branch which is directly responsible for dealing with subversion and anti-government activity. Needless to say, much of its work is confidential and this has led to criticism of it as a kind of secret police. It bears no comparison with the political secret police of totalitarian countries, however, and supports the government in power, irrespective of its politics. Public enquiries into its methods have always cleared its name.

Television can help in solving crimes. *Day and Night*, a current affairs TV programme, aims to bridge the gap between the police and the public. One of its items, *Crime Line*, enlists the help of people in tracing stolen property or people who are wanted.

FOR INVESTIGATION AND DISCUSSION

1. Do you think police forces should be relieved of duties such as road traffic to concentrate on the prevention of crime and arrest of criminals? Give reasons for and against this.
2. Discuss whether British police should carry arms openly as they do in some other countries. You could also organise a debate on this.
3. Compare the British police force with those of other countries. What do you think are the advantages and disadvantages of the British police system?
4. Contact your local Police Schools Liaison Officer. Invite him to speak to your group on the work of the police force.
5. Find out as much as you can about the various jobs done by your local police force. In what ways can the ordinary citizens help their local police?
6. Why does a policeman's job sometimes make him unpopular with people?
7. What aspects of police activities in your own locality bring them into contact with people in a useful way?
8. Using local newspapers, find out about what the police have been doing during the past few weeks. How many cases affect young people, older people, real criminals?
9. The police have sometimes been accused of brutality when dealing with violent demonstrations. Give your view of this and say how you would deal with such demonstrations if you were a policeman or policewoman.
10. (a) What are the big problems over law-enforcement which are likely to face society in the future?
    (b) What kind of training may the police officer get at Bramshill that would help in tackling them?

6

SENTENCES AND TREATMENT OF OFFENDERS

Different societies have many ways of dealing with offenders, and in trying to make sure that their rules or laws are kept.

In some societies ridicule plays a part, as with the Eskimos and their taunting songs or the Mbuti pygmies of Africa (see *Groups and Communities* by Paul Mathias). Public opinion has a strong influence over the maintenance of law and order. That is why many people dread getting into trouble with the police or appearing in a court. They are afraid of what people will think of them and the possibility of losing their jobs.

Revenge
Punishment for breaking the law has taken many forms. The traditional way has been to punish by way of revenge. For example the punishments laid down for the Jewish people were along the lines of retaliation: 'eye for eye, tooth for tooth, hand for hand, foot for foot' (Exodus 21:24 and elsewhere in the Old Testament part of the Bible). Revenge killings may take place where a member of a tribe has been murdered by someone of another tribe, in some parts of the world. Among the Tswana people of Africa physical retaliation is allowed in cases of assault, particularly on a woman.

It was an ancient Saxon custom in Europe to declare a wrongdoer an outlaw and allow him to be killed by anyone. In Saxon Law 'bot' or compensation could be paid to the victim of violence. For example, it is stated in the laws of King Alfred of Wessex:

> If the great toe be struck off, let twenty shillings be paid him as bot.
> If it be the second toe, fifteen shillings; if the middlemost toe, nine shillings.
> If the fourth toe, six shillings.
> If the little toe be struck off, let five shillings be paid him.

Some very serious offences were 'botless' and those committing them were declared outlaws and so might be killed. If the bot was not paid, the offender would become an outlaw.

King Alfred (871–900) laid down that his laws were to be applied equally to rich and poor, and he kept a close watch over his courts to make sure that judgements given were just. The right of direct appeal was allowed.

Treatment of offenders
In recent years there has been less emphasis on punishment by way of revenge. There is more concern for giving the offender treatment that will help him to keep the law. Society has of course to be protected and that is a strong reason for giving penalties for breaking the law and for removing criminal from society by imprisonment. However, the offender will be back again in society at some point so that it is in everyone's interests to give him treatment that will help him to go straight and stop committing crime.

Several factors therefore have to be considered over the sentences given:

1 Whether the penalties imposed on the offender are morally right.
2 Whether they protect society by acting as a deterrent.
3 Whether or not they should contain an element of vengeance.
4 Whether society needs to be protected by offenders being imprisoned.

50

An old form of punishment: the treadmill

In passing sentence, rehabilitation of the offender is now a strong consideration in many countries. Attempts are made to reform criminals wherever possible, both while in prison or through other means. Public opinion is divided on the question of capital punishment, which many still regard as just. Although flogging and the death penalty have been abolished in Britain, some think severe punishments should be given in cases of deliberate violence. They think such punishments are just and will help to stop criminals from committing acts of violence. Others argue against this. What do you think?

SENTENCES IN BRITAIN

When a person brought to court has been found guilty, there are several alternative ways in which the magistrate or judge may pass sentence. The nature of the offence, the circumstances and character of the person found guilty, all influence the sentence given.

In a few cases a magistrate or judge may pronounce *Absolute discharge* with no punishment or treatment being given. This is usually when the person brought to court has obviously had such a severe shock that he or she is not likely to get into trouble again.

Conditional discharge means that the offender is discharged on condition that he keeps the law for twelve months. If he commits another offence during that time, then he is likely to be punished for the first crime too.

Another alternative is *binding over to keep the peace*. In this case an offender has to pledge money that he will come up for judgement when called upon. He may be brought to court again (even without committing another offence) if he has failed 'to keep the peace'—that is to be of good behaviour. Fighting, or unruly behaviour, is one example of an offence being dealt with in this way. *Fines* may be given in some cases. In deciding whether or not to impose this form of punishment, there are several factors the court has to bear in mind: the circumstances of the offence and the offender's previous records; whether it is against the interests of society or the offender that he should not have some other form of sentence. In fixing the fine, the income of the offender and his expenses are taken into consideration and this influences the period of time in which he is allowed to pay it.

Suspended prison sentences. Where a sentence is imprisonment for two years or less, it may be suspended. It will not be enforced unless another offence is committed, when it would automatically have to be served as well as any additional sentence for the new offence. One of the reasons for a suspended sentence is that going to prison might cause a person to lose his job and entail hardship to his family.

Where it is thought that the prisoner would profit by being given a chance, this sentence is likely to be given. Another factor which is taken into account is the nature of the crime.

51

Probation Service in Britain

A probation order may be given to a person of any age. In deciding on this, the court has to consider the possible danger to society of a person being on probation instead of being detained and weigh that against the chances of the offender being able to respond to this attention while remaining free.

Common requirements of probation are:

to be of good behaviour and to work

to notify the probation officer of any change of address

to keep in touch with the probation officer as he may instruct and to receive visits from the probation officer at the offender's home.

An offender has to be under the supervision of a probation officer for a specified period of not less than one and not more than three years.

Probation would not be given to those from whom society needs to be protected, or who have committed serious crimes.

In Canada a variety of community resources are called on to assist the probationer. Volunteers help in the correctional programmes which usually involve a one-to-one relationship not possible for an officer with many cases.

The object of probation, as of other methods of treatment, is to re-establish the offender in the community. The service was pioneered as a voluntary service between 1876–1907, in both religious and legal fields in order to find some good alternative to some of the very harsh and destructive penalties imposed at that time by the criminal code. Those undertaking the work proved that often a person could be saved from a continued life of crime and instead be an asset to the community. In the USA and the United Kingdom this idea spread and in 1907 a Probation System was set up in the UK.

Probation officers try to understand people in their care, their background, family difficulties and obligations, and help them to meet these. Sometimes they can help offenders to understand the nature of their wrongdoing. Often an offender may not see at all why he is wrong, or why he should change his ways. A probation officer may help him to face up to his responsibilities and be able to explain legal procedure and rights to him. This often relieves an offender of a great deal of anxiety. If a person on probation commits a crime and comes before the court again, the probation officer will often speak on his behalf, if he considers that the person has tried to do better but perhaps old habits or old companions have had too strong a hold. If the person is sentenced to imprisonment, the probation officer will still keep in touch, and sometimes may help by seeing his family or over any personal worries.

A case was given in the BBC series *The Lawbreakers* (Programme 10) of a boy who began stealing partly for the money to spend on things he wanted, and partly for the excitement. He was in a boring job. He was asked if he felt any concern for those he was stealing from and he said that at first he did and minded about this, but later on he got used to it and it just became a job. The excitement wore off after a time.

He was caught several times and went to

prison. The longest sentence was seven years for burglary. Then for his next offence instead of imprisonment he was put on probation. About that time he met a woman he was later to marry. She knew his past record but also that he wanted to go straight. He knew she obviously would not put up with any more dishonesty, so decided he must change. But later when his second child was born and he fell out of a job, he did the only thing he knew to get money: housebreaking. He was caught and sent to prison. When he came out, he had no work so stole again. His wife wanted nothing to do with him: this was the second time since their marriage. But the probation officer believed in him, that he really wanted to live honestly, and talked to his wife. Finally, he was allowed out on parole after serving one year of his four-year sentence and his wife took him back. At last the pattern of stealing was broken.

Imprisonment: its aim
In the words of the Prison Rules:

> the purpose of the training and treatment of convicted prisoners shall be to encourage and assist them to lead a good and useful life.

How far this is possible depends on the prisoner, his criminal history, whether he wants to be trained or treated in this way and his response; it also depends on the availability of accommodation which needs both to provide essential security and facilities for training and treatment.

British prisons
There are some 60 prisons in England and Wales and six in Scotland. Many of these are closed or maximum security prisons. These were built mainly in the nineteenth century when their main purpose was to keep prisoners locked up and unable to escape. They are very overcrowded and this

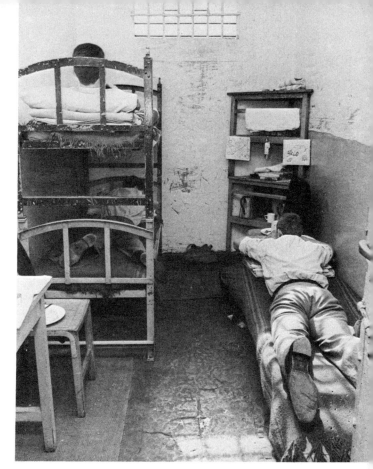

An old-style of prison cell

A typical cell in the rebuilt 'C' wing of Lewes Jail which contains 146 cells.

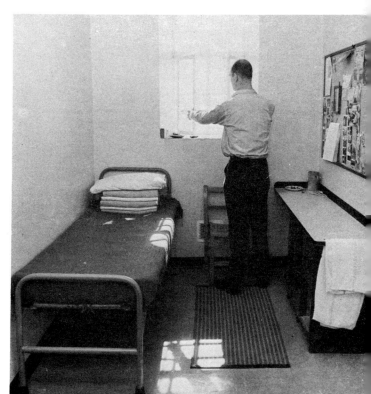

53

Prisoners at Leicester Prison in the brick-laying shop, helping to build another prison

Prison officer chats to civilian instruction officer in charge of the typing class at Hill Hall Prison, Essex

Section of Dartmoor Prison ('D' Wing)

makes attempts at rehabilitation and pre-paration for a return to normal life in the community difficult. Small cells intended for one person are often occupied by two or three. This gives the more dangerous and hardened criminals even more opportunity to exert a bad influence on others—especially when the cells are occupied for a lot of the prisoners' time.

Only a vast expenditure of public money would enable the reforms necessary in the prison service to be carried out. Not only are prisons overcrowded but they are badly understaffed and the prison officers themselves are overstrained. Many new prisons need to be built, not only to relieve the overcrowding but also to enable new methods to be introduced, prisoners of different kinds to be kept apart and more rehabilitation to take place.

There are some *open prisons*, where the prisoners are given maximum freedom and where it is felt they are able to be more easily rehabilitated.

Prisoners often welcome a link with society that is provided by prison visitors. Some take the opportunity to study and are allowed to choose books. The prison chaplain may play an important role in some cases.

A *remission of a sentence* may be given for good conduct. This is one of the ways of ensuring that discipline will be kept.

Parole. Sometimes prisoners will be released 'on parole'. The Parole Board was set up by the Criminal Justice Act of 1967 to advise the Home Secretary on release of prisoners under licence to assist in their easy return to normal life.

A Local Review Committee consisting of the governor, local magistrate and probation officers will consider which prisoners are suitable for this and make recommendations to the Parole Board whose members include psychologists, criminologists, judges and after-care experts. They have to be satisfied that the prisoner, by his response and attitude in prison, wants to

A Review Board interviewing a prisoner to see if he is suitable for transfer to an open prison or for home leave

become a law-abiding citizen and that there is every hope that, with the help of his supervising officer (usually probation officer) he will be able to do so. There is always, of course, the chance that a prisoner may try to 'con' people into believing that he is reformed and sometimes serious assaults and acts of violence have been committed by prisoners on parole. So one has again to weigh the good of the prisoners against their possible danger to society.

After release from prison
On leaving prison a small sum of money is given to all prisoners serving sentences of over three months, and they receive travel warrants or fares to their destination. They are offered after-care help from the probation and after-care service, but it is entirely their choice (unless released on licence on parole) whether they wish to accept this.

Psychiatric treatment in prison service hospitals
Where someone found guilty of a crime is 'of unsound mind' he will be treated in a psychiatric hospital, on instructions from the Home Office. There are also facilities within the prison system for treating offenders with particular disturbances such as drug addiction and alcoholism.

Alternatives to prison

A strong desire to keep people out of prison and various moves for reform have led to many alternatives to imprisonment being possible, such as Community Service Orders and Suspended Sentences.

Experiments have been carried out with Community Service Orders. The offender must be 17 or over, and his offence one that would otherwise have meant imprisonment. The judge may say that as an alternative he can do so many hours' work that is of value and help to the community. Up to 24 hours a week is the maximum sentence. Usually the offender is able to carry out the community service on a part-time basis, perhaps at weekends. His work is supervised by a probation officer and if he does not turn up for it or carry it out satisfactorily, he goes back to court and may be fined up to £50 and ordered to do the work. If he still does not, the order may be revoked and a sentence of imprisonment given instead. If his case was originally tried in the Crown Court, he will have to appear again before the Crown Court.

Young offenders

Young offenders in Britain are persons under the age of 21: they are divided into two groups one of 17 and over and the other of under 17. Young offenders under the age of 17 are tried in the Juvenile Court, and may not be sentenced to imprisonment. They may be detained in a detention centre (if 14 or over) or remand home for short periods. Detention centres are a means of treating young offenders for whom a long period of residential training away from home is not felt justified or desirable, but who cannot be taught respect for the law by payments of fines and for whom probationary care is not felt suitable. Often those who go to these centres have offended several times already. The discipline is strict but the staff are trained to take a personal interest in the young people and to make a real effort to find out why they go wrong and to help and encourage them. Work forms an important part of the treatment, and it is designed to create a habit of consistent effort and also to stretch the young people to the limit of their ability: along with domestic work they are given constructive jobs such as making sports nets, concrete moulding and work on the farm. Much of the work is repetitive but it is productive and the high standards encourage the boys to get a sense of achievement. (At present there are no detention centres for girls.)

Community homes

In 1973, as the result of an Act of Parliament, the old system of Approved Schools was replaced by a scheme of community homes. These pay considerable attention to social training—that is, the art of living in a community, with other people. There are separate house units and many respond to this by showing consideration and care for their house and its equipment. Psychiatric help is given where necessary. In the teaching, special attention is given to crafts and to preliminary training in such trades as building, agriculture and catering.

HM Borstal, Stockheath. General view of cell block.

56

Borstal training

A sentence of Borstal training may usually be passed only by a Crown Court.

A person sentenced to borstal training may be detained for up to two years from the date of the sentence. The average period is about 14 months.

It is for young offenders who are considered unsuitable (or are too old) to go to a community home and who need a longer period of remedial treatment than can be given in a detention centre.

Each boy or girl sentenced to Borstal treatment is sent first to an allocation centre when a careful study is made by specialist staff of his (or her) history, character and capacities and he is then sent to the training Borstal best suited to his requirements. There is a wide variety of Borstals and also taken into account are the offender's record and degree of criminal tendencies and activities; his physical and mental condition; his comparative maturity; whether his training is better in open conditions or whether he requires close supervision.

The aim is the all-round development of character and capacities. The kind of work varies from place to place. Most Borstals have farms as well as workshops and in some the boys go out daily on their own to work for neighbouring farmers, or other employers. The girls get particular training in home management.

All offenders get the chance to go home once during their training for five days. This is to give them a chance to re-establish relationships and to help them back to the realities of life in the community.

Probation and after-care

Release from a Borstal is followed by a period of supervision by the probation and after-care service for up to two years from date of release. While the offender is in the Borstal the probation officer is encouraged to visit him or her. This personal interest and care is very important.

Boys from an open Borstal helping at a Cheshire Home

Committal to the care of a fit person

As well as coming under the care of a Probation Officer, an offender under the age of 17, who is guilty of an offence for which as an adult he might be imprisoned, may also be committed to the care of a fit person, sometimes a local authority, or a relative or private person who is thought suitable. In selecting the person, the court must take into account whether they are of the same religion as the young offender.

The 'fit person' is given the same rights and duties as a parent and has the care and custody of the child or young person. This often means that a child is removed from bad surroundings and given a better chance.

Boys in a Borstal Institution in Kenya watching a film *Freedom* which shows how tribal unity may be achieved

Where a child is in the care of the local authority, he or she may be boarded out with foster parents or go to a children's home.

Attendance Centres

These are usually organised by police officers in their own time for boys under 17. Attendance is usually two or three hours each Saturday and the main activities are physical training, hobbies and lectures. The aim is to develop interest and personal standards.

FOR INVESTIGATION AND DISCUSSION

1 Find out what you can about ancient methods of trial by ordeal, and how much they are used in some societies today.
2 Find out more about Saxon Law and why the death penalty was not often given.
3 Find out about laws under King Alfred, the system for his courts and his close supervision of the judges to make sure the sentences were just.
4 Are fines sufficient deterrent for some offences, and if so which offences?
5 Napoleon brought a new system of laws to France in the early nineteenth century. Find out about the Code Napoleon and the laws of France today.
6 What is your attitude to people who have been to prison?
7 What problems face people who go to prison, while they are there and when they are released?
8 Find out what you can about the following organisations:

> Howard League for Penal Reform
> Justice
> National Association for the Care and Resettlement of Offenders (NACRO)
> Radical Alternatives to Prison (RAP)
> Salvation Army's work with prisoners, or that of similar religious bodies

9 Discuss the suitability of various sentences and punishments for different types of crime. How can one 'make the punishment fit the crime'?
10 What is being done, and what more might be done to rehabilitate prisoners?
11 Find out what you can about community service for young people instead of prison sentences in several countries.
12 Find out what you can about the kinds of sentences imposed in several other countries and compare them with those in England.
13 Organise a debate on the motion: 'Capital Punishment (hanging) should be re-introduced for murder'.
14 What changes do you think ought to be made to prisons in Britain? Find out what you can about prison conditions in France, USA, USSR or other countries.
15 Find out as much as you can about life in a borstal.

7
THE LAW IN ACTION

Learning about the law

Although most people pick up quite a lot of knowledge about the law from other people, from newspapers, television and other ways, there is much of which they are completely unaware until they come into contact with it.

There are three particular reasons for learning about the law (a) because you may be committing an offence against it (b) because you have got into trouble with the law, or someone has committed an offence against you and you need to know the legal position (c) because you are buying a house, making a will or are in another situation where you require the help of an expert.

A basic principle of English Law is that 'an accused man is innocent until he is proved guilty'. Another is that 'every man is presumed to know the law'. This means that the plea can never be made that a person did not know that a particular law existed. This is because this reason could always be given as an excuse for disobeying a law, even when it was not true. The principle exists to protect the public from wrongdoers who might otherwise get away with anything. It is therefore important to find out about some laws which may affect you. For instance, under (a) it is useful to know up to what ages certain activities are not permitted by law. This diagram gives some interesting examples:

(1975)	Below	12	13	14	15	16	17	18	19	20	Years 21
You cannot legally: Smoke in public						•					
Buy fireworks			•								
Buy a pet		•									
Vote in elections								•			
Become an M.P.											•
Marry without parents' consent								•			
Marry with parents' consent						•					
Drive a moped of 50 c.c.						•					
Drive a motorbike							•				
Drive a heavy lorry (over 3 tons)											•
Drive a car							•				

Whether people have got into trouble, or whether they want to find out about something, the Law can appear very bewildering to the ordinary person. Yet there are few people whose actions don't bring them into contact with the Law. Take, for example, a young couple wanting to buy a house and raise a mortgage; someone letting or renting a flat; a boy with a motor-bike or car; or someone buying goods on credit and then not paying for them.

Buying a house

Buying a house, for example, involves two distinctly different approaches for the average person. The transfer of ownership of the land and house, and the mortgage by which the house is bought.

The legal title must be transferred from the seller to the buyer in a way that ensures that the buyer becomes the complete owner. What is more, the buyer wants to make sure that there will be no unexpected claim of any kind of this land after he has bought it: that the deeds of the property are in the language of the law, free from incumbrances or covenants. This means a right of some other person to right of way over the land, or special use of it, or to build next to it or something similar. To protect the buyer, his solicitor or other legal representative arranges for enquiries to be made by conducting Land Registry searches and examining the deeds. He also checks with the local council about any future planning, such as a motorway or other development that may affect the property. Sometimes after enquiries have been made, the purchaser may agree to buy the property in spite of such disadvantages, but at least he has been made aware of them.

Conveyance

When it is certain that the legal title is free, a document is drawn up known as a deed of conveyance, more usually as a conveyance (it conveys the ownership of the property from one person to another).

It is set out as follows:

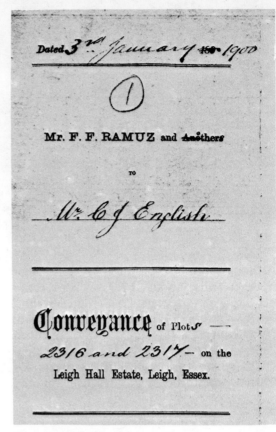

The cover of a Conveyance document

The parties
This states clearly the people concerned in selling and buying the property and gives their addresses.

Recitals
This states the purposes of the deed, the events leading up to it and to show the previous history of the title.

Receipt clause and operative words
This states the money involved, that is the purchase price and the operative words which actually transfer the property from the seller to the buyer.

The parcels
This is an accurate description of the property to be conveyed.

60

Collage of Building Societies Association's leaflets

A mortgage

Most people have to borrow some money from a building society, a local authority, or an insurance company by means of a mortgage in order to buy a house.

A mortgage is an arrangement by which property is transferred by the owner to another person as security for the loan of money. If the loan is not repaid the property may be seized.

Where a house is bought, a legal document known as a mortgage deed is drawn up by which a sum of money is lent to the purchaser and a promise is given to repay the loan by a certain date, often by regular amounts being paid over a specific number of years. Interest is charged on the loan so it is an advantage to pay the mortgage off as soon as one's income allows. The most usual mortgage is with a building society when the money, plus interest, is repaid by monthly instalments over a period of about 20 or 25 years. The building society usually requires an intial lump sum to be paid and this helps in obtaining a mortgage for the remainder of the money. If the repayments lapse, the lender may sell the property to repay the outstanding loan. The law tries to protect the person who borrows the money, and the lender may only do this with permission of a court of law. This permission is only given if no attempt is made to repay the loan. Even when permission is given and the lender seizes the property, after the loan has been repaid and also any legal expenses, the balance of the money received for the property goes to the borrower. The mortgage deed is drawn up by the solicitor (usually the building society solicitor does this) and the building society keeps the property deed until the money has been repaid.

Eviction

Many people live in rented accommodation. If they are threatened with eviction, whether for non-payment of rent or for other reasons, they may be in fear of finding themselves without a home. The Rent Act of 1974 gives protection to those in furnished accommodation while those who live in unfurnished houses and flats are also given protection by the courts. No one may be evicted without an order of the court and the court investigates the circumstances thoroughly before granting it. If an eviction order is granted, it is the duty of the local authority to provide accommodation, although sadly this often means hostels and families being separated. While people get more security of accommodation, some people may become more reluctant to let rooms because of this.

Law and the motorist

An enormous number of people drive motor cars and motor cycles today and so come into contact with the law.

The law states that a motor vehicle must have a road fund licence, its driver must have a driving licence and the vehicle must be insured, at least against third party risks.

Let us consider an imaginary case. Jim Bower has a motor cycle of which he is very proud, although he hasn't much money to run it.

While riding it one day, Jim was stopped by Police Constable Martin because it appeared to be very noisy and he thought that it might have a defective silencer. PC Martin asked Jim for his driving licence and certificate of insurance. Jim had neither. When his licence and insurance ran out he did not have the money to renew them, so he just didn't bother. The policeman then noticed that his road fund licence had also expired. He had let that go too. Jim was charged with:

1 Driving without a driving licence.
2 Driving a motor vehicle without a road fund licence.
3 Driving while uninsured.
4 Having a defective silencer.

In due course he received a summons to attend the local Police Court. There the magistrates listened to the evidence of PC Martin and heard what Jim had to say. He was found guilty on each charge and fined a total of £40 and disqualified from driving for a year.

Jim felt that he had been very severely treated and could not see that he had committed very serious offences. He did not realise that had he knocked someone down and injured them, or damaged another

vehicle, the people concerned would have received no damages or compensation because he was not insured. Even if he had been insured, no insurance company would pay out if his road tax had not been paid.

This is a relatively minor case, as most motoring offences are. However, what happens when a person is involved in something much more serious?

David Evans was driving home one night after doing business with a customer. He was a representative for an engineering firm. He had been entertaining his customers and had quite a lot to drink. He took a right-hand bend much too fast, lost control of his car and hit a car coming from the

opposite direction. The driver of the car was killed. David was charged with:

1 Manslaughter.
2 Causing death by reckless or dangerous driving.
3 Reckless and dangerous driving.
4 Driving while under the influence of drink.

He was charged at the local Police Court where the evidence was heard. The magistrates decided that there was a *prima facie* case (a case 'at first sight'). Because his offences were serious he was remanded for a Crown Court. There his case was heard by a judge and jury and he was represented by a barrister.

He was found guilty on all charges and

was sentenced to three years' imprisonment and disqualified from driving for five years. This was a disaster to David and his family since it would mean losing his job. With the advice of his barrister and a solicitor, he decided to appeal against the sentence. His appeal was heard by the Court of Appeal, Criminal Division, where three judges decided to allow it. His sentence was made a suspended sentence of two years and he was disqualified from driving for one year only. This meant that he would only go to prison if he committed a further offence during the three years and with his wife driving the car for him for a year he could keep his job.

Failure to pay a bill

We have been considering how the law works in criminal cases but many people are involved in simple civil cases. What happens if Leslie Grey and his wife buy a large amount of groceries on account from Ray Dean's shop over a period of several weeks and fail to pay for them? Ray Dean's patience is exhausted after trying many times to obtain the money and he decides

to take legal action. He puts the matter in the hands of his solicitor and the following takes place:

1 A letter is sent to Leslie Grey requesting payment within seven days.
2 If there is no response a default summons is taken out and details are filed at the office of the County Court.
3 A summons is usually served by the Court Bailiff.
4 If there is no response within 14 days, judgement is given for Ray Dean.
5 Leslie Grey may respond within 14 days by entering an admission agreeing to the debt, a defence claiming that it is incorrect, or a counter-claim.
6 If a defence is filed, the County Court Registrar may give judgement, or decide on a trial.
7 If there is a trial it is heard by a County Court judge.
8 If judgement is given for Ray Dean, there are several means of his recovering the money owed. A Warrant of Execution is the usual method. This gives the bailiff of the Court authority to seize goods or property of the debtor if the money is not paid, although the threat is usually sufficient. Another legal method is an Attachment of Earnings Order which instructs the debtor's employer to deduct the money owed from his wages or salary. The other legal orders are given for much larger debts.

These various examples of how the law works all normally involve people in approaching a solicitor and sometimes engaging a barrister. This can be expensive and, in addition, most people are confused by the law.

Neighbourhood Law Centres

Because of this, Neighbourhood Law Centres have been set up as an experiment. They have small permanent staffs of solicitors and legal executives and usually a number of volunteer helpers at evenings and weekends, who include barristers, solicitors, typists and students. Here people can obtain the advice and help they need. The Government is now actively encouraging these Law Centres and more are being set up.

Legal Aid symbol

Citizens' Advice Bureaux can also help people in difficulty by giving legal advice, and guiding them along the right lines.

Legal Aid

Under this system people who do not have much money can have help towards paying for a solicitor or barrister. The Statutory Legal Aid Scheme under the Legal Acts of 1949, 1964 and 1972 enables any person to claim legal aid and advice. The Criminal Justice Act of 1967 made Legal Aid available also in criminal cases.

Most solicitors operate the New Legal Aid scheme. You can find one by:

* visiting the nearest Citizens' Advice Bureau—the address is in the telephone book. The people there are very helpful and if you think you may have difficulty in fixing an appointment, ask them if they'll arrange it;
* asking friends, relations or your trade union representative;
* going straight to a solicitor's office which displays the Legal Aid symbol shown here;
* finding solicitors' addresses at court office, or at a Law Society Legal Aid Office, or in the 'Law List' which most public libraries have;
* writing to:

  New Legal Aid
  PO Box 9
  Nottingham NG1 6DS

FOR INVESTIGATION AND DISCUSSION

1   The Law is noted for its special language, which is not always easily understood. Find out the meaning of the following terms:

Writ, intestate, lien, precedent, fee simple, estoppel, affidavit, pleadings, decree nisi.

2   Williams is charged with having killed his neighbour Rogers, having been found standing over the body with a knife in his hand, although he claims he found the body and the knife nearby.
  (a) What would he do to defend himself against the charge?
  (b) In which courts might the case be heard?
  (c) If he had no money, what might he do?
  (d) Describe the proceedings in any one court.

3   Find out about the Rent Act of 1974 and discuss the points for and against it (a) as regards the tenants (b) the person letting. Discuss also whether it is likely to cause a shortage of rented accommodation since the rights of the person letting to give the tenants notice are more restricted by the Act.

4 Find out how one becomes:
    (a) a Solicitor
    (b) a Barrister
    (c) a Crown Court Judge
    (d) a Lord Justice of Appeal
    (e) a Probation Officer
    (f) a Policeman
    (g) a Prison Officer
    (h) a Justice of the Peace (JP)
    (i) a Legal Executive.

5 Write a short account of the work of one of the above and the importance of their role in society.

6 Construct and carry out a survey to find out what ordinary people know about the law. You might include the following questions:
    (a) Do you believe the law is fair and that you would get a fair trial if you went to court?
    (b) What changes were brought about by the Theft Act of 1968?
    (c) In what circumstances are fines imposed? How are they paid in the cases of children and young offenders?
    For method of survey see *The Teachers Handbook for Social Studies* by Paul Mathias (Blandford).

7 We are affected by the law daily without really noticing it. This is particularly so with reference to bye-laws, that is laws made by local authorities or public bodies applying only in certain places and circumstances.
    (a) The next time you travel on a bus find out how many laws and regulations are displayed in notices. See if any are on your bus ticket.
    (b) Look on the platform at a railway station and see how many bye-laws you can find.
    (c) Go to a public park or recreation ground and see what notices are there.

8 Find out and make a list of any recent changes in the law or in the Courts. What changes are being planned at the moment?

9 Look in some newspapers, national or local, and see if there are any reports of any law cases. Make a note of the type of case, the court and any interesting points about them.

10 Find out what kind of legal matters are dealt with by the following organisations:
    Justice
    Citizens Advice Bureau
    Legal Aid
    Neighbourhood Centres.

11 Are there any laws affecting people between the ages of 14 and 21 which you think should be altered? If so, which ones and for what reasons?

12 How are consumers protected by law?

13 Find out about recent laws about the protection of wild birds, pollution, or any other subject that interests you.

8

LAW IN A CHANGING SOCIETY

Quite often today there is the demand to know and to have one's rights. For this, an understanding of the legal position is important. Several examples of cases where there are laws which define one's rights have already been given.

Constitutional law has been referred to in Section 3. It may be of interest to know some of people's duties as well as their rights under the British Constitution.

The rights and duties of the citizen
Loyalty of people to the Queen is always expected, although an oath of allegiance, or loyalty, to the Queen is only made when someone takes up special duties, or when someone of another nationality becomes a British subject. This allegiance carries with it certain duties. For example:

1 A citizen must serve the State, if necessary in the Armed Forces, if called upon to do so.
2 All citizens have the duty to maintain law and order and to assist the police.
3 All citizens must give evidence in court if called upon to do so.
4 Every citizen has the duty to register births and deaths and to take part in any census.

These are some of people's constitutional duties which help to ensure their rights. These rights are numerous. Here are four examples:

1 All citizens are protected from arrest and imprisonment without trial by the writ of *Habeas Corpus* (see p. 10).
2 Every citizen has the right to private property which can only be taken away with his permission. If Parliament passes an Act which involves the State taking over private property it is assumed that consent exists, since the House of Commons was democratically elected. This might happen in wartime and through Nationalisation Acts.
3 Citizens are guaranteed freedom of discussion and freedom of the Press, but the laws of libel and slander apply.
4 Citizens have the right of free association and of public meetings, unless the purpose of that association or meeting is itself unlawful.

The basis of these rights is the principle of English Law that everybody is entitled to do what he pleases so long as it is not forbidden by law.

Civil liberties
In spite of constitutional protection which the citizen has, the question of civil liberties is still of some concern because as government administration has become larger and more complicated, so people's ordinary rights have, in some cases, been cut down through such things as delegated legislation and special tribunals. Delegated legislation can sometimes lead to powers being passed on to official bodies which allow them to interfere with an individual's freedom. Although this is for administrative convenience and usually works well, it can be abused.

There are also some non-government bodies which possess the power, if not always the authority, to interfere with personal freedom. Examples of these are Private Monopolies, Trades Associations and Trade Unions. A Union can take action against a member who is considered to have

66

offended, in such a way that his whole livelihood may be affected.

In any country there is need for constant vigilance to see that freedoms are not eroded. This is sometimes difficult because of the changing attitudes of public opinion, or some sections of it.

Changing attitudes

When people, who are now middle-aged, were children, authority was generally accepted more or less without question. Children were 'seen and not heard' and young people rarely criticised the views and opinions of their elders. The class structure was more rigid and clearly defined and it was more readily accepted.

This has changed a lot for various reasons since the Second World War. There is now less readiness to accept authority and people are much more ready to challenge the older standards and ideas.

This is more to the good than to the bad but apart from the fact that some people believe that the changes have gone too far,

it inevitably brings problems. It is much more difficult to maintain law and order, or even an ordered society, when authority is being challenged. We often make difficulties for ourselves by challenging accepted standards and in extreme cases suffering can be caused to many innocent people. Nevertheless, changing attitudes may eventually cause changes in the law.

Increased violence—new measures

At the time this book went to press, certain types of violence were increasing, especially in the cities. People became afraid of going out at night because of violent attacks in the London Underground and other railway stations. There were attacks on London bus crews especially those running late in the evening. One busman was killed and the effect was dynamic throughout the transport service. Many busmen refused to take their buses out, especially at night, without some protection. This led to alarm buttons being fixed to many of London's buses. There was some doubt whether the law as

Plan to beat bus rowdies.

Assaults increasing

Scare train drivers miss out

BOMB POLICE CHECK TUBE TRAVELLERS

Alarm system

Tube 'hell' man is fined £85

Muggstation

'd easy

Bus thugs

prey on Tube, say

BOYS ACCUSED OF KILLING TRAIN GUARD

Transport Police

it then stood made this devise illegal. The law has now been altered. This is a case where changing circumstances make a change in law necessary. New remedies are needed as fresh situations arise. We have already seen changes necessary over the question of arming the British police in some circumstances.

This raises many questions. Some people blame society and lack of opportunities for some of the delinquents and also their background. The threat to and disregard of authority which is true of today's society may account for much of it.

Public co-operation

We need to bear in mind the point in Section 1, that society must have social rules to function effectively, and to protect the interests of the weaker members. For this public co-operation is needed.

Without respect for law and order society may disintegrate. This is what happened to the boys in *Lord of the Flies*. Are people capable of understanding the larger issues involved by their wilful breaking of the law, and by their failure to support it for the common good?

FOR INVESTIGATION AND DISCUSSION

1   Crime in cities all over the world is increasing. Discuss ways in which the community may help in preventing and combatting crime.
2   Attacks on transport workers in cities may cause great hardship to ordinary people through some buses and trains not running late at night for fear of attack. What measures would you suggest for dealing with this situation?
3   Society has been changing during the last 25 or 30 years. Has the law changed sufficiently to keep pace? What changes in the law would you like to see?
4   Do you think that the greater freedom for young people and reduced respect for authority is to be welcomed or not?
5   By studying your local newspapers see how much violent crime there is in your area. List the offences and, where possible, the sentences given, and compare them.
6   Do you think that sentences given for violent crime are sufficient or suitable? Discuss and make your own suggestions.
7   Look at the rights and duties of the citizen as listed in this section. How do you react to them? Add any which you think should be included.
8   'Rights and duties' suggest that freedom is only possible with a sense of responsibility. Where do you think that there is a lack of responsibility today?
9   What is a crime? Name five crimes which you consider to be anti-social. Choose one of these. Find out whether the rate of this crime has fallen or risen recently, give possible reasons and say what sort of punishment ought to be given to people who commit it.
10   Find out about a citizen's right of arrest. Give any examples of where this right has been used.
11   Give examples of recent changes in laws in Britain. Suggest reasons.

GLOSSARY

absolute discharge: the charge has been proved but there is no punishment.

Act: law made by Parliament. Also called a Statute.

advocate: one who pleads the case of another in a court or tribunal; a barrister or solicitor.

affidavit: a written statement in the name of a person who signs and swears to it.

Bill: a law in the process of being made. It is called a bill while passing through Parliament. Later it may become an act.

Capital punishment: punishment by death.

charge (1): the accusation, made formally, that an offence has been committed.

charge (2): in property law a charge is a form of security for the payment of a debt or carrying out an obligation, consisting of the right to receive payment.

circumstantial evidence: evidence which appears to be correct and relevant by the circumstances of the case.

conditional discharge: discharged subject to following the instructions of the court and dependent on good behaviour.

contempt: failure to comply with orders of a court; lack of respect for a court.

contract: an agreement, binding in law, made between two or more persons or groups. It must contain an offer, an acceptance and some sort of value, known as 'consideration'.

conviction: being found guilty.

counsel: a barrister (generally practising barristers).

court of chancery: this was the court of equity presided over by the Lord Chancellor.

custody: being under arrest and kept in the cells or in prison awaiting trial.

decree nisi: every decree of the ending of marriage is in the first instance a decree nisi not to be made absolute until after six months, unless the court orders a shorter time. (Literally—a decree unless some reason is produced why it should not be made absolute.)

defendant: a person against whom an action, information or other civil proceedings (other than a petition) is brought; also a person being charged with committing a criminal offence.

delegated legislation: when the power or authority to carry out certain actions is given by the government to local authorities or other bodies.

deterrent: something which is likely to dissuade someone from doing a particular thing. In law, something which is likely to prevent the law being broken.

diminished responsibility: considered to be not fully responsible for actions.

Director of Public Prosecutions: the official who advises private prosecutors and chiefs of police on prosecutions and undertakes prosecutions on behalf of the State in important cases.

equity: fairness or natural justice. A fresh body of rules by the side of the original law, founded on distinct principles, bringing moral considerations to bear.

evidence: all the legal means (except for mere argument) which tend to prove or disprove any matter of fact, the truth of which is submitted to the court or tribunal.

extradition: delivering a person who has committed a crime in one country by the authorities of another country in which he has taken refuge to the authorities of the country where the crime was committed.

habeas corpus: a writ or command to a person who detains another in custody and requires him to produce or 'have the body' of that person before the court. (Acts of 1679 and 1862.)

in camera: in closed court with no members of the public present.

indictable offences: the more serious crimes normally tried by judge and jury in the Crown Court.

indictment: a written accusation of one or more persons of a crime.

judicial: to do with a court of law or with judges.

juvenile: legally, one who is under 18 years of age.

maxim: a legal maxim is a rule of legal conduct expressed as a saying, usually in one sentence.

perjury: telling lies in evidence when on oath.

plaintiff: one who brings an action at law.

pleadings: written or printed statements delivered alternately by the parties to one another, until the questions of fact and law to be decided in an action have been established.

precedent: a judgment or decision of a court of law given as an authority for deciding a similar set of facts: a case which serves as an authority for the legal principle embodied in its decision.

prima facie case: a case in which there is some evidence in support of the charge or allegation made in it; a case at 'first sight'.

Queen's Evidence: to give evidence in support of the prosecution when one of the accused.

remand: to send a prisoner back into custody while further evidence is obtained.

remedy: in law, the action ordered by a court to put right a wrong.

rolls: in ancient times, records were written on pieces of parchment stitched together so as to form a long continuous piece, which was rolled up when not in use.

special tribunals: special courts given authority to investigate certain actions or disputes, e.g. a tribunal to inquire into the reasons for a particular strike.

statute: an Act of Parliament.

statute book: the collections of Acts of Parliament as a record of those in force.

sureties: people who will guarantee by a sum of money the accused's attendance at court.

territory: land ruled by a particular nation or state, including the air above and some of the sea surrounding the land.

treason: an act against the Crown or state: particularly assisting an enemy of the state.

trusts: associations between persons, based on confidence, by which property is vested in or held by the one person, on behalf of and for the benefit of another.

writ: a document in the Queen's name and under the seal of the Crown, commanding the person to whom it is addressed to do or stop doing some act.

GENERAL REFERENCES

Encyclopaedia Britannica

Gloag and Henderson, *Introduction to Law of Scotland*, W. Green & Son

Kiralfy, A. K. R., *The English Legal System*, Sweet & Maxwell (3rd edition 1967)

Osborn, P. G., *A Concise Law Dictionary*, Sweet & Maxwell (5th edition 1964)

Phillips, O. Hood, *A First Book of English Law*, Sweet & Maxwell (6th edition 1970)
The Sentence of the Court HMSO

FOR FURTHER READING AND INVESTIGATION

Alderson, J. C. and Stead, P. J. (ed.), *The Police We Deserve*, Wolfe Pub. Co. 7th edn, 1973

Bates, Frank and Coull, James W., *Questions and Answers on the Law of Scotland*, W. Green & Son, 1970

Belsen, Dr. W., *The Public and the Police*, Harper and Row

Firth, Raymond, *Human Types*, Sphere/Abacus, 1975

Golding, William, *Lord of the Flies*, Faber, 1964

Helm, P. J., *Alfred the Great*, Robert Hale, 1963, pp. 108–117 (For Assignments 1–2 in Section 6)

Leigh, Mellor, J., *The Law*, EUP, 1974 edition (Teach Yourself Series)

Mathias, Paul, *Groups and Communities*, Blandford, 1974

Miller, Jack, *Life in Russia Today*, Batsford, 1969

Perry, Gordon A., *Police and Police Services*, Blandford, 1974

Pettifer, Ernest W., *Punishments of Former Days*, EP Group of Companies

Purcell, W., *British Police in a Changing Society*, Mowbrays, 1974

Solzhenitsyn, A., *The Gulag Archipelago*, Collins/Fontana, 1974

First Circle, Collins, 1968/Fontana, 1970 ⎫
Your Parliament, EP Group of Companies ⎬ for the passing of a bill
Filmstrip on *The Story of Parliament* from ⎭
EP Group of Companies

See also Resource Lists in *The Teachers' Handbook for Social Studies* by Paul Mathias, Blandford, 1974

Addresses
The Law Society, 113 Chancery Lane, London WC2
The Building Societies Association, 14 Park Street, London W1A 4AL

ACKNOWLEDGMENTS

Acknowledgment and thanks are due to the following for their help in supplying or checking information: The French Embassy, Home Office, Law Society, Law Society of Scotland, London Transport, Metropolitan Police, USA Embassy, Building Societies Assn.

Photograph acknowledgments

Kenneth Beare, p. 57 (bottom); Camera Press, p. 6 (bottom), p. 28, p. 29, p. 34, p. 43, p. 47, p. 48 (top); Columbia-Warner, p. 15; C.O.I., p. 54 (bottom—2), p. 55, p. 56, p. 57 (with Home Office permission); Peter Cooper, p. 46 (bottom); Granada TV, p. 33; Keystone Press, p. 26, p. 27, p, 32, p. 46 (top); International Court at The Hague, p. 12 (2); Commissioner of Police of the Metropolis, p. 44, p. 45; Law Society, p. 35, p. 36 (top left Clareville Studios, other 3 and p. 36 Sam Lambert); Mary Evans, p. 45 (bottom); Ministry of Correctional Services, Canada, p. 52; Netherlands National Tourist Board, p. 11; Press Sss., p. 53, p. 54 (top)—Home Office permission; The Scotsman, p. 41 (by permission of the Lord President); Society for Cultural Relations with the USSR, p. 17; Collages by Marion Mills; Diagrams and cartoons by McCaffrey & Sharp.

Cover, Camera Press, BBC, David Williams, Camera Press; Centre: Cameron Johnson sketch of the Goddess of Justice. (In one hand is a balance in which to weigh the good and bad actions of people. In the other a sword to show her power of punishing the wicked. Over her head is a bandage to represent the impartiality with which she listened to people.)

INDEX

absolute discharge, 51, 69
Acts of Parliament, 22, 24, 69
Adversary and Inquisitorial Systems, 38
advertisements, 20–1
advocate, 42, 69
After-care help, 55, 57
ages up to which some activities are not allowed, 59
Alfred, King, 50
alibi, 40
Appeal Courts, 30, 31, 63
appeals, 50, 63
arrest, 10, 37, 45
assault, 23
Attachment of Earnings Order, 63
Attendance Centres, 56, 58
authority, 67–8

bail, 37, 38
bankruptcy, 29
barristers, 33, 63
binding over, 51
Blackstone's *Commentaries*, 19
Borstals, 56, 57
building societies, 61

capital punishment, 51
Carbolic Smoke Ball advert., 20
Central Criminal Court (Old Bailey), 30
citizen's rights and duties, 66
civil cases, 63, 64
    liberties, 66
committal to care of fit person, 57
community homes, 56
Community Service Orders, 56

compensation, 23, 26
conditional discharge, 51, 69
conduct, rules of, 7, 23
conscience, 7
    court of, 22
contract, 20–1, 23, 29, 34, 41, 69
conveyance, 41, 60
counsel, 36–8, 40
Court of Appeal, 31, 63
    Coroner's, 38
    County, 29
    Crown, 30, 37, 38, 39, 40
    High, 30, 32, 36, 39
    Juvenile, 28–9, 56
    Magistrates, 28, 37, 40
    Metropolitan Magistrates, 28
criminal action, case study of, 39–40
criminal record, 40

custody, being kept in, 10, 37, 69
of children, 10, 57
customs, 7, 19–20

damages, 23
death penalty, 51
debts, 29, 63
defamation, 21, 24
defendant, 34, 36, 39
democratic governments, 14–15
detention centres, 56
Dicey, Albert, 10
divorce, 10, 24, 26, 29
domestic relations, 22, 24
driving offences, 8, 62–3

English legal system, 19–26
Equity, 19, 22, 69
eviction, 61–2
evidence, 66, 69
in Scotland, 42

fines, 51, 56, 62
flogging, 51
freedom of the individual, 14–15, 66
freedoms, basic, 14
French magistrate, 29
police, 48

Habeas Corpus writ, 10, 15, 66, 69
Hammurabi's code, 8
house purchase and sale, 34, 59–61

Icelandic fishing dispute, 12
indictment, 37, 39, 40, 69
inheritance, 9, 41
International Court, 11–12
INTERPOL, 48

Judges, 20, 21, 32
at International Court, 12
Puisne, 32
juries, 30, 38–9, 40
jury, trial by, 37
Justices of the Peace, 28

Land Registry, 60
Law, Case, 19
Civil, 23
Common, 14, 19, 21, 22
Constitutional, 22, 66
Criminal, 22–3
Roman, 14, 19, 41
Rule of, 10, 17
Scottish, 41–2
Statute, 19
Law Society, 34

laws, changes in, 14, 26, 68
making of, 22, 24, 25
moral, 7–8
purpose of, 26
reasons for, 7
religious, 8, 10
sources of, 19–20
variations in different societies, 9,
10, 15
Legal Aid, 38, 39, 64
Legal executives, 33, 34, 63
systems, 10, 14–18
Lord Chancellor, 31, 32
Lord of the Flies, 6, 7, 67

marriage, 10
Master of the Rolls, 31–3
matrimonial law, 24, 26
McAlister v. Stevenson, 21, 24, 42
mortgage, 22, 61
motor vehicles, 62–3
murder, 8
Muslim laws, 8, 10

negligence, 21, 23, 24
Neighbourhood Law Centres, 63
New Scotland Yard, 44, 49
nuisance, 24

oath, evidence on, 40
of allegiance to the Queen, 66
ownership, 9, 10

parole, 53, 55
Peel, Sir Robert, 45
perjury, 8, 69
Petty Sessions, 28, 30
plaintiff, 34, 36
plea, 37, 60
police, arming of, 43, 44, 48, 68
clashes with demonstrators, 45–6
organisation in Britain, 44
in other countries, 47–8
Police College, Bramshill, 46–7
precedent, 8, 19, 20, 21, 69
Prevention of Terrorism Act, 1974,
26
prima facie case, 37, 62, 69
prisons in Britain, 53–5
alternatives to, 56–7
psychiatric treatment in, 55, 56
Probation Service in Britain, 52–3, 57
in Canada, 52
in USA, 52
property, 9, 10, 23, 29, 41
deeds, 60, 61
protection, 26, 61, 66

public opinion, 26–7, 50, 51
punishment, 7, 50, 51

recorders, 30, 32
Registrar, Court, 29
rehabilitation of offenders, 51
remission of sentence, 55
Rent Act of 1974, 61
retaliation, 50
re-trial, 39
rights of individuals, 10, 66

Scottish Legal Profession, 42
Scottish Legal System, 41
Police College, 47
slander, 24
solicitors, 34–6
Solzhenitsyn, Alexander, 17, 48
Statute Book, 22, 69
summons, 36, 63
suspended sentence, 51, 56, 63

territorial rights, 8, 9
theft (stealing), 8, 39–40
Theft Act of 1968, 26
Tolley v. Fry, 21
tort, 21, 23, 24, 34
totalitarian governments, 15, 48
treadmill, 51
trespass, 23
trial, stages of, 36, 37, 40
trusts, 22, 23

United Nations, 12
USA, 9, 15, 19
CIA, 48
Federal and State Laws and Courts,
15–16
National Guardsmen, 43
police, 43, 48
USSR, 9, 17
KGB, 48
Federal and State Courts, 16
People's Courts, 16–17
State Arbitration, 16–17

verdict, 37, 40
violent crime, 43, 44, 67

Wales, law of, 19
Warrant of Execution, 63
wills, 29, 59
witnesses, 29, 36, 40
writ, 36

Young Offenders, 56, 57